19 TRUE STORIES OF
GRIEF AND MENTAL HEALTH JOURNEYS

YOU CAN, YOU WILL

Julianne Williams
Along with 18 Inspiring Women Authors

ISBN: 978-1-960136-10-7

Table of Contents

INTRODUCTION

You Can, You Will is written for people whose lives have been affected by mental health, grief, and difficulty. Nineteen sacred stories of overcoming experiences that could have destroyed the very lives of these women are shared to provide inspiration that life can and does change, that there are solutions to every struggle, and wholeness and happiness can be found. After reading this book, the readers will have strategies to make the changes in their life for healing and joy.

The authors in this book share deep and personal circumstances to bring healing to others who are walking in their shoes. These women have lived through some of the unspeakable events we hear about or may be a part of what we have lived - suicide, physical, emotional and sexual abuse, relationships crumbling before our eyes.

The theme you will embody from these stories is no matter what, You Can and You Will. No matter what you are going through, these authors will give you the resolve to press forward, find YOU, and create a life you love. You are not alone. Our goal is to normalize the conversation around grief and mental health to free others of the shame and stigma that have been wrongly placed on those who suffer.

Know that you can get through anything! And, you are never alone.

Julianne Williams

MPH, LHNA, Certified Grief Educator

http://linkedin.com/in/julianne-williams-1aa76917
https://www.facebook.com/BraveEnoughCommunity
https://www.instagram.com/brave_enough_community_/
www.juliannewilliams.com
www.conizo.com/shop

Julianne Williams is a mom, 3-time international best-selling author and Certified Grief Educator. She holds a B.S. in Developmental Psychology and a Master of Public Health.

A licensed nursing home administrator, she rose to the President of the second largest skilled nursing care company in the US overseeing over 320 locations with 30,000 employees.

After leaving skilled nursing care, she formed a healthcare consulting company and is currently on the Board of Directors for a hospice care company. She also serves on several national boards in the healthcare arena.

Julianne hosts a show named "Step Into Your Life" on Fenix TV through Apple TV, Roku, and Fire TV available in 100 countries.

Her mission is to help people heal from grief and build a life they love.

THROUGH THE DARKEST DAYS

By Julianne Williams

"Everything seems impossible until it's done"
—Nelson Mandela

On my knees, again, praying for help. Desperate. Overwhelmed. I'm not sure I can make it this time.

I have made it through so many hard life experiences and circumstances, but sometimes, the accumulation of daily life and all that goes with it feels like too much. We spring into action, get our wits about us—or whatever you want to call it—when there is a tragic or difficult situation. It's almost like we know we have to pull ourselves up by our bootstraps and find solutions to get through or survive. Each time I had to overcome difficulty, even when it seemed complicated, I knew there would be a path forward. I also knew it may not turn out how I expected. But I did know that somehow, someway, I would survive.

But today, I am frankly overcome with daily living. Those difficult circumstances have put my entire life in a trajectory I don't want or like. How can I face all of the responsibilities and stress of managing life?

Losing my husband to suicide and raising my children on my own was not my plan. Being left in a precarious financial situation due to his mental illness was not my plan. Being taken to court by my late husband's father to get partial custody of my kids was not my plan. But through tears, pain, and sorrow, I forged ahead to save my and my children's lives.

I endured many months of hopelessness while all of this was going on. I couldn't understand how my "perfect" life flipped into my biggest nightmare. I knew in my heart of hearts that there would be a light at the end of the tunnel, even though I didn't know when that light would shine again.

Why? From day one on this planet, I learned to become a fighter. Being born with a congenital heart defect that would limit my life span, I had to persevere long enough to have the surgery that would ultimately save my life. Because I struggled to breathe from what would be considered "normal" activities for other children, I found ways to compensate. I could not crawl, so I would scoot across the floor. When I turned blue from the lack of oxygen, I would instinctively squat down so my heart could pump more efficiently and I could catch my breath.

When the doctors told me, even after my surgery, that there were limitations, I still fought to find how I could create the life of my dreams. I wanted to be like everyone else, and feel like I was normal. I already felt odd with a scar on my chest, certain medication requirements, and continued doctor appointments. I was never able to stop thinking about my health. I also could never stop thinking about how my health was still potentially limiting my ability to fulfill my greatest desires. This gave me the drive to be solution-oriented. Because I wanted the fullest life possible, I was continually looking for strategies to overcome.

And I did!

Even though I had a healthy dose of fear, I knew there had to be a way. When my husband and I decided we wanted to be parents, I consulted my doctors on the risks and how to minimize the chance of a bad outcome. I discovered there were steps I could take to better prepare my body for me and my baby. I had to make the choice to follow the instructions and advice. It was all about choice. I did the same thing when I wanted to run half marathon races. I went to my cardiologist to get his support and advice. He gave me specific parameters by which to abide so I could reach my goals. Again, I had to choose to be disciplined and brutally honest with myself. That all seemed very possible. I met each obstacle with determination and overcame them to achieve the outcome I desired.

But there I was, not sure how to deal with the daily stress I faced. Even the routine tasks felt formidable.

You see, while I knew there would be a light at the end of the tunnel regarding the "big" things, I didn't see how or when there would be any glimmer of hope around the physical and mental challenges of my day-to-day life. Between being a single, only parent which meant overseeing meals, bath, homework, school clothes, field trips, sports and other extra-curricular activities, maintaining my home, paying bills, preparing meals, doctor appointments, attending church, and more, plus being a traveling executive in the healthcare world that was on call 24/7, the days were long. I felt like my life was a continual juggling act. And, I couldn't drop any of the balls because all were essential to survival and ultimate success.

I didn't share with anyone that I was engulfed by busyness to the point of exhaustion, not as patient with my children as I wanted to be, and simply going through the motions of life. Most days, all I cared about was getting through that day, praying nothing more would happen and there would be no "hiccups." Everything was scheduled so tightly that leaving shoes at home or not quickly hopping in the car could totally disrupt the ability to be on time. This infused every event and errand with pressure on all three of us.

There had to be a better way. And so I am sharing what it took me years to figure out…

First, I had to recognize that I was placing most of the stress on myself with unrealistic expectations. I had this notion that I had to be perfect and that what others thought of me mattered. It took courage I didn't know I had to identify what I was doing for the sake of "appearances," to be admired, or to prove something to someone else. Finding the fortitude to follow my heart, not the outside world, was the challenge I had to overcome. As I let go of things one by one, I found that I didn't feel any different about my success or confidence. I could be me, and that was good enough.

Next, my first concern had to be me and my children. Their spiritual life, emotional development, and physical health had to be the focus. Anything outside those areas had to be put on the back burner. I had to take the time to truly set my priority, not only for me but for the children. Of course, that meant I had to be very clear on what was important. Not to others but to my family. I made a list of all the demands, appointments, and activities we were involved in. I simply crossed out all of the items that would not propel us to a place of happiness or growth. Honesty with myself was the most difficult part of this task. I found some things I felt were important for the wrong reasons, and some commitments would not ultimately benefit the three of us as we healed and found a life after the death of my husband and their father.

Staying close to God was also imperative to remind me that my children and I had a purpose, and that no one could derail what we were to bring to the world. The book of Ephesians 2:1-10 raises the point that we are "made alive in Christ." Those words represented to me how I was dead while trying to follow the ways of this world rather than what Jesus had planned for me. Specifically, in verse 2:10, which says, "For we are God's handiwork, created in Christ Jesus to do good works, which God prepared in advance for us to do." In other words, God put me here for a purpose, and I am living my life to fulfill that purpose, not one placed on me by me or even myself.

Lastly, you have to take small steps every day. It can't all be done at once. Make a list of what you would like to accomplish each day. When you see those items crossed off, you will feel a sense of pride. As our faith in ourselves grows, it motivates us to keep moving forward. And, all of a sudden, those small changes turn into big shifts.

When you are in those times when the day seems overwhelming, step back and remember you are not alone. If we are all honest, we all have hard days and hard times. By acknowledging we want our situation to change, we can—we will—find a life full of happiness.

Crystal Neil, CFP®

Edward Jones
CERTIFIED FINANCIAL PLANNER™

https://www.linkedin.com/in/crystal-neil-cfp%C2%AE-39274b139/
https://www.facebook.com/crystal.neil.18
https://instagram.com/serenitythai?igshid=YmMyMTA2M2Y=
https://www.edwardjones.com/us-en/financial-advisor/crystal-neil

Crystal Neil is a mother of three beautiful girls Taylor, Danielle, and Nicole. January 19, 2002, she and Brian eloped during a snowstorm. She is a CERTIFIED FINANCIAL PLANNER™ for Edward Jones. They homeschool their girls. Crystal is very active within her community. She is the head coach for girls' varsity soccer and the sprints coach for the track team. Crystal started the Indy Genesis track and XC teams for her daughter Taylor. She serves on the track board for Indy Genesis. She is a ministry partner and loves her small group within Grace Church in Camby. She enjoys time with her family, reading, sports, traveling, sunshine, and nature. She is passionate about children, mental health, faith, and being the light and the change we need to see in this world. She advocates suicide prevention and improving mental health resources and care.

KEEP MOVING FORWARD

By Crystal Neil, CFP®

I remember a time in my life when my greatest concerns were the girls' homework getting finished, unexpected car repairs, stresses at work, and the usual life hassles. This was also a period when I avoided my feelings and could never admit my greatest fear. I was honestly blessed beyond what I ever dreamed or imagined for my life. I was a mother of three beautiful girls, Taylor, Danielle, and Nicole. I had a career I enjoyed and was passionate about, I was part of a magnificent small group within a fantastic church, and I was blessed to be actively involved in my local community as a coach and board member with our homeschool sports group. Our lives seemed to be the healthiest they had ever been before our greatest devastation.

Taylor Nicole Neil was a bright light who captivated the room's attention no matter where she was, how she was dressed, or what mood she was in. She was larger than life from when she was born on June 29, 2003. Tay accomplished more in 18 and a half years while battling borderline personality disorder (AKA, BPD) than most individuals in over 100 years. She was intelligent, a gifted artist, a talented dancer, a soccer athlete, and an accomplished runner in Cross Country (AKA, XC) and track. She also participated in cheerleading and Muay Thai boxing.

She graduated from the Hoosier Youth Challenge Academy (HYCA) in December 2020. She received her high school diploma from Excelsior Academy in May 2021 as a homeschool graduate. Her first job was at Chick-fil-A, where she worked for 18 months. She worked a short time for Taco Bell before leaving to attend an accelerated program through HYCA. After graduating from HYCA, her resume afforded her the Director of Events & Planning for Dye's Walk, a country club in Center Grove. When she accomplished all she could with the country club, she became a barista with Starbucks. She was employed with Starbucks at her passing.

She was passionate about animals, mental health, sports, faith, astrology, and the metaphysical realm. Taylor was the kind of person you could trust with any secret, no matter how dark, out of character, exciting, or breaking news the secret was. She would not judge you or reject you. She was fiercely protective of her family and close friends. Tay would lose a competition or personal record to help the underdog or fallen competitor. She would go out of her way to help others and fight for justice. She was hilarious, quirky, creative, inventive, and a trendsetter for her time. Taylor was unapologetically authentic and eclectic in so many ways. She lit up the room wherever she went. She was planning to go to college and study psychology but had a strong interest in law. She could win a debate all day long, arguing the grass was blue when we know the grass is green. She had a hypnotic approach to getting what she wanted and swaying your opinion. Taylor was an extraordinarily charismatic individual who will be missed beyond words.

Despite all these wonderful qualities, characteristics, and attributes, her life tragically ended way too soon and in the traumatic manner of suicide. Taylor is a victim of her brain turning against her and a system incapable of helping her. Even though I have so many unanswered questions, thoughts, fears, and unknowns, I know without a doubt Tay passed in a single moment of chaos, and it was not intentional or meant to happen. She did not want to die; she wanted her pain to stop. She desperately wanted that moment of chaos to end. In a single moment, her brain was broken and she was completely incapable of any rational thoughts, powerless to signal for help.

Our brains are designed by nature to protect us and survive, and the "flight or fight" kicks in instinctually. Other parts of the brain shut down to ensure our survival. When somebody dies by suicide, the flight or fight portion of the brain is temporarily disabled. The brain cannot signal to get help or fight for survival. Suicide leaves ripples far beyond anyone's recognition.

Taylor's loss was no different.

My greatest fear my entire life was failure. When I became a mom, my greatest fear I could never vocalize was failing my children. Being a mom is the most awesome responsibility; there is no calling in life more important than being a mother. I did not want to fail my little girls. I prayed daily for God's grace and guidance, wisdom, and discernment. While battling Tay's BPD in the deepest and darkest moments, I feared failing her. I cried and begged God not to let me fail her and to transfer her pain to me. I would gladly bear her pain. I longed for her to beat this struggle. I wanted her to be a living testimony for others who struggle and to give hope. I wanted her to live a healthy and happy life by her standards. I wanted her free from the agony she endured daily.

Sadly, that day never came. I was working late on Wednesday, December 22, 2021 to wrap up loose ends before Christmas. I was preparing for extended time off. I began receiving multiple texts from Dani and a call from Niki saying she thought Tay was dead. There it was, my worst fear coming true. I failed. I failed my Tay and my daughters because they're living in pain right now. This was not supposed to happen; it goes against the laws of nature.

I am their momma; I am supposed to protect them. I carried them all inside me, nursed them, healed them repeatedly, hugged them, and dried their tears. I dedicated my life to protecting, loving, and raising them to be lights in this world, yet I failed.

More than my fear of failure, I lost my baby girl, my girls lost their sister, and our family is broken beyond recognition. The Neil family died 12/22/21 and is forever scarred. The days following that moment are a blur. If I'm being honest, the entire year following her death is a fog. Grief brain is real.

I know I cried daily for the better part of the year. I remember the first day I did not cry, maybe around month nine. I remember thinking I was proud for a moment because I went tear-free for one day! My body freaked out because pain and suffering were normal, and now a day of peace meant something was wrong. Keep in mind, I am somebody whose "Joy" (if you have ever seen the movie "Inside Out" by Disney) is always in control of my headspace. I can write an entire book on how deep and immense this pain is, but I only have one chapter in this book.

Within a few weeks, I knew I needed to face my feelings, heal my trauma, and learn to somehow live with my grief and pain. I knew I must keep moving forward because I still have two beautiful girls who need me. I would not lie down and wait for death to consume me. Every morning when my eyes would open, the pain my heart felt was more significant than language could articulate. The pain extends far beyond the heart; it consumes the entire soul. Body, mind, and spirit are mutilated beyond comprehension. When you ask, "How are you today?" You know those who say, "I'm vertical." I was not one of those people. But I knew I had to take the steps and get to a place where I was glad to "be vertical."

I began listening to the podcast Totally Got Out of Bed. I found it by doing a Google search. It is a great podcast by two extraordinary women who also lost a child to suicide. I burned through the two seasons in no time. People do not understand that when you experience great trauma, your amygdala is overstimulated to extreme measures. It shuts down various portions of your brain until you are just in survival mode.

Multiple studies confirm that individuals who experience emotional trauma show similar brain scans as individuals suffering from traumatic brain injury. The major difference is that those suffering from trauma are expected to continue their normal lives. Society needs to begin looking at mental health the same way we look at other diseases.

Before losing Tay, I was an avid reader and could not listen to audiobooks or podcasts. I could not focus on listening to them. After her loss, I could no longer read books; I could only listen to audiobooks and podcasts. "Totally Got Out of Bed" was helpful, but I needed more.

Track season was in full swing, and I struggled because this was Tay's sport. I helped create the Indy Genesis track program for Taylor. She was supposed to help coach this season, so it was difficult for multiple reasons. One of my favorite families mentioned a friend was looking for guest speakers for her podcast. She had lost her husband to suicide and asked if I would be interested. Ah, yes, please!

I was blessed to be a guest and share Tay's story on "Brave Enough", and I began listening to Julianne William's podcast. Julianne's podcasts, books, love, and support have been pivotal in my healing. She provides me with a safe platform to share my and Tay's stories. I was once told one of the best therapies for healing trauma is learning to share your story in a safe way that does not trigger you. Julianne gave me this gift. She shared her story without ever meeting me. She is a blessing and will always be one of my soul sisters.

People began reaching out to me, thanking me for speaking up. Many others would ask me for help and resources. So many people were struggling, but they began feeling empowered to tell their stories and now felt less alone. I was inspiring others by being open, raw, and honest. I was motivating others to come forward. I became hopeful this could prevent others from suffering our same fate.

Mental health in the United States is subpar. I know it has evolved significantly, but we can do better. The mental health care, support, and resources available are a huge disappointment, especially for those struggling and suffering. I discovered how difficult it was to find organized resources and quick help for those suffering and in need. So, I began keeping a running list in my Notes app; a list of books, websites, numbers to call, trauma therapists, and any resource that may be useful for someone's toolbox.

Podcasts were helping me, so I began making a list of podcasts for suicide survivors. I ran across "The Leftover Pieces" by Melissa Bottorff-Arey. This was a podcast that spoke to me. Melissa is a mom who lost her son to suicide, and her podcast is ongoing and dedicated to suicide survivors. She always provides an eclectic mix of experts, guests, and specialists on her podcast. Her podcast is one of the best for those suffering from trauma. She even provides well-organized show notes with details from her guests.

Melissa was also starting a class called Grief to Growth, designed to help grievers heal from their trauma. I signed up for this as well as her all access support group. This is a support group for forward-thinking suicide loss survivors. Being a part of this group of ladies provides me with a safe space to share the difficulties of daily life as a grieving mom. I can also share successes as other moms move forward and learn about tools that work for them. We all need a tribe of peers who understand our suffering.

I am lucky enough to still have my bestie from childhood. Alyson and I have been best friends since we were in diapers. Her family moved to a different school district after kindergarten, but we have always remained close. Despite going through periods in our lives where we do not connect as often as we would like (life happens), we pick up like we never missed a beat whenever we connect. When Alyson learned of

Tay's passing, she scheduled her family's vacation to Indiana. She knew I could not go through this alone. Whenever I call her, no matter the hour, she answers and listens. She is always ready to 'throw down' and go after someone for talking smack. And, she always sends me random pictures of animals (she's a veterinarian). Tay loved animals.

My daughters and I began seeing a therapist specializing in trauma and EMDR therapy within two months after Tay's passing. I scheduled the appointment initially for my girls. Eventually, I began seeing Heather (our therapist) as well. I will never forget discussing a concern with one of my girls, and Heather assured me. She asked me what I do to care for myself. I could not answer this because coaching and volunteering for my community were not an acceptable answers. She told me taking care of the girls when I first called was a concern, but she knew from our first visit that I needed the most help. This shook me to my core. She told me nothing was wrong with me other than my deep trauma and how important it was to heal so I could continue being a good mom.

One of the last tools I want to share is "Wooville." Tay always had a strong foundation of faith. She was baptized twice: once in first grade and again as a junior. She began expanding her faith in Wooville to seek additional healing for her mental health. You can find crystals, seashells, rocks, stones, and earth elements of various sorts all through her room. I remember days when Tay would run down the stairs with enthusiasm because it was raining during specific periods, and she was going to collect that special rain. She would make moon water to clean or drink, and she had all kinds of dances for celebrations.

I have felt a strong connection to Taylor and found immense healing by embracing the various aspects of Wooville. Crystal healing, aroma therapy, and connecting more with nature are a few of the aspects I practice daily. I see a natural healer regularly who uses Reiki and Native

American medicinal treatments. Cranial sacral massage therapy, tapping, and music are also tools I keep in my toolbox for therapy. Body, mind, and spirit all need love and attention to live happy lives and heal from trauma.

I never wanted to be on this devastating journey. I pray I am honoring God and evolving into my best self through this pain and suffering. My pastor's wife, Ruthann, always says, "God doesn't waste pain." I know now more than ever I have a divine purpose of helping others who are struggling and spreading awareness about grief, mental health struggles, and suicide prevention. I hope by sharing a small piece of my beautiful Taylor's and my stories, you find tools for your toolbox and the courage and inspiration to keep moving forward through your journey.

Stephanie Dauble

The Payne Street Collection
Author

https://www.linkedin.com/in/stephaniedauble/
https://www.facebook.com/sdauble
https://www.instagram.com/daubleganger/
https://stephanie.nyc/
https://medium.com/@stephanie.dauble

Born and raised in Detroit, Stephanie is a tenacious and resilient leader whose experiences, natural wit, and zeal for life inspire her to process difficult times and trauma in uncommon ways. She is the author of a weekly blog titled Stephanie Dauble: Memoirs of a Junkie's Daughter, From The Payne Street Collection. Stephanie is on a mission to share how navigating grief with grit and gratitude can lead to unexpected fulfillment, lasting change, and extraordinary beauty. Stephanie bravely confronts a lifetime of overcoming generational pain triggered by addiction and suicide and boldly declares her strength exists because she's a junkie's daughter, not despite it. She shows up fully expressed and brings a fair, soft, non-judgmental grace to her stories. Stephanie's take on transcendence through trauma is a distinctive blend of humility and promise that encourages us to approach difficult times through a lens of gratitude.

THANK GOD MOM'S A JUNKIE

By Stephanie Dauble

Mom invites me into the bathroom to watch her shoot up, and I'm thrilled it's finally happening. Usually, she's holed up in there for hours while I wait in the hallway. I've even fallen asleep on the floor outside the bathroom, waiting for her. Once on my birthday, she must have blacked out because it was too late to have pizza and cake by the time she opened the bathroom door. Mom always misses everything.

It would feel like the days she drags my little brother, sister, and me to the heroin house, where she makes us wait for hours on a sticky wet mattress with the other drug kids — except this time, I get to be a part of it. Inside our small, stagnant bathroom, Mom takes a seat on the closed toilet and I sit beside her on the bathtub's edge. It's a miserably hot July day, with no fan, window, or ventilation; Mom's thin, greasy hair sticks to her sweaty forehead.

I studiously watch her delicately and deliberately tap white powder from a small yellow envelope into a neat little pile in the middle of a spoon she grabbed from the kitchen. I won't dare talk to her amid such important work. She ignites her lighter under the spoon until the little white pile becomes liquid. Vigilantly, she sets the spoon on the vanity counter while she prepares her arm. She's mastered the art of arm preparation, clenching the two ends of a tourniquet with the few decayed teeth she has left to keep it tight and in place. She then sticks the needle into one of the only veins on her arm that hasn't collapsed, tilts her head back, and closes her eyes. As the drugs race through her body, she looks like she's in heaven. And in hell.

I feel like an invisible witness to her ritual and wonder why she invited me in. I was thrilled to be included, but now I'm getting bored and antsy, so I lie down on the floor at her feet as I wait for her to notice me. Eventually, she comes to, and without saying a word, she reaches down for my arm and brings it into the light to have a better look. She then uses her thin pointer finger to trace a vein. For years, she's been jealous of my veins. She's told me so.

"I'm not doing heroin." My voice trembles from holding back tears. More silence. I can tell by how she looks down at me with her vacant, blue-turned-black eyes that I've crossed an invisible line. I've made her angry. Like the Grim Reaper, she silently lifts her skinny arm and points at the door — my signal to get out. She locks the door behind me. In the hallway, I doubt myself. Perhaps I should have done the drugs with her? But I didn't, and now I'm an outcast. I

place my hands on the bathroom door. "Mommy, please don't be mad at me. I'm sorry." I'm ten years old. That's the last time she asks me to join her for anything.

I remember Mom before heroin. She was a good mom, but she seemed sad most of the time. I remember the ambulance coming to our old house and carrying her out on a stretcher after she overdosed on prescription pills. I'm not sure how many times exactly, but from the time my little brother was three years old, he wanted to be an ambulance driver when he grew up to "be with Mommy."

Mom was hanging on by a thread, more than anyone knew. After my little sister, her third child, was born in the late 70s, severe post-partum depression set in. She knew she was in big trouble and actively sought treatment, but the doctors back then dismissed her, and the diagnosis for what she was feeling was that it was "all in her head." She tried everything to feel better, including convincing my dad a new home in a new town would help. New scenery would do our growing family good.

We moved to a Cape Cod-style house with a white picket fence on a road named Payne Street. There are a couple of apple trees, a little white bridge over a babbling brook, and huge lilac shrubs that are said to supply an amazing scent come springtime. But after a few months in our new house, she doesn't feel better. In fact, she feels worse. She resorts to contacting her cousin, who lost a leg in a recent motorcycle accident. To ease the pain, her cousin recommends heroin. It only takes one hit, and Mom's hooked. Almost at once, our world is turned upside down. From the outside, it remains idyllic. On the inside, it's hell.

On the inside, it's kids raising kids. Mom drains our bank accounts and uses what little money we have for drugs. We come close to pricking ourselves with used needles kept in random drawers. It's the early 80s and the start of the AIDS epidemic, so we're paranoid we'll "catch it" like the junkies, prostitutes, and unfortunate blood transfusion recipients we see on TV. Many mornings before school, Mom makes us pee in a cup so she can pass it off as her own at the methadone clinic. Dad is trying his best to keep things afloat, but it's a full-time job to keep Mom from self-destructing. He's in an impossible position — he's damned if we stay and he becomes her enabler, and damned if he goes. In the 80s, moms typically get full custody of their kids, so he can't leave with us, either. The best he can do is manage her and put everything else on me and my siblings. Everyone's hungry. Every surface is sticky, even the carpets. I'm exhausted, embarrassed, and ashamed. Our friends aren't allowed to come over; I've heard their parents don't want them at our house. I can't blame them. I don't want to be here either. In all, it will be 3,650 days of hell on Payne Street.

In my family, many generations have succumbed to the perils of mental illness, addiction, and suicide. It's a seemingly unbreakable generational curse. When Mom was a teenager, she lost her own mother to suicide. By all accounts, Grandma dove headfirst into a huge cluster of jagged concrete chunks that formed a seawall of a popular lake near Detroit. She broke her neck and died instantly. Her suicide was a very public and embarrassing scene. Mom seldom speaks of it but tells me that on the day it happened, Grandma wore a floral-print house dress my mom had sewn for her in a Home Economics Class. Mom took Grandma's choice in clothing as a sign of blame, which began her downward spiral and what would become a lifetime of failed suicide attempts and addiction. A part of my mom drowned in the lake with Grandma that day. And the generational cycle continues. Still haunted by Grandma's demise fifteen years later, my mom decided to take me and my little brother and sister to the same spot where Grandma took her final dive. Grandma took a piece of her daughter down with her, and now our mom was determined to take her kids down with her too.

Mom is driving with one reluctant forearm draped over the steering wheel while a cigarette with a long, hot ash dangles precariously from her persistently chapped lips. I'm in the front passenger seat, worried that hitting a bump will make the hot ash break off onto her bare thigh. My little brother and sister sit in the back seat, chit-chatting in a whisper. I keep looking over at my mom to see if she'll look at me, but she doesn't. Or she won't. The profile of her right eye looks like a shark's eye — dark and empty. Maybe she's out of sorts again because she just got home from the halfway house. Regardless, I'm happy she's home, even if she is ignoring me. When she's in treatment, she only gets a weekend pass to come home once or twice over the course of several months. She's broken out of the halfway house and escaped a few times, but I think it's an approved visit this time.

Mom finally rolls down her window a smidge and starts a new cigarette. The warm breeze that flows in my direction feels good. The first few puffs of her new Winston waft in my direction, and I love the smell. Her smoke means she's home. I look out the window, and I know where we are. Mom has pointed out this location before. This is where

Grandma died. Fifteen years to the day, and in the same spot Grandma dove headfirst into a pile of concrete, this little drive by the lake's edge is no coincidence. Mom drives in circles alongside the lake, back and forth, while I watch her attentively. I'm old enough to grasp what's happening but not old enough to do anything about it. I'm terrified, but it's best to stay silent. Finally, she pulls the car away from the lake and heads home. History doesn't repeat itself; she doesn't end her life or ours.

The gravel crackles under the tires as we finally round the corner on Payne Street. Dad's waiting for us — looking exhausted, sweaty, and grateful we're home safe. Apparently, she told Dad she was taking us to buy new shoes and pre-cell phones. He had no way of knowing where we were. We'll never know why Mom changed her mind. Perhaps, unlike Grandma, she has a mustard seed of hope. At the halfway house, she has a reputation as someone who always tries. She's broken, but she's not a monster. She's hurt, afraid, addicted, and always trying to improve. Her resilience is admirable, and against all odds, I'm learning good lessons from a junkie.

With drug addiction, it's the chemical stronghold on the body and mind that destroys lives, not the soul of the body it inhabits. And over the years, I've learned when dealing with Mom's anger, mistreatment, abuse, and fury — none of it is because of me. I may be in the path of a storm, but I'm not the reason for the storm. If we separate the illness from the individual, we can understand, heal, and overcome our pain. I was born to the perfect mom for me. If I was meant to have a different mom, I would have. If God wanted to spare me from trauma, he would have. If I wasn't meant to know darkness and despair, I would have been raised in the light.

We can find purpose in our darkest hours. It's a long-standing belief of mine that was put to the ultimate test on my brother's 44th birthday.

After years of healing and self-discovery, I believed the worst was behind us, for me and my family. But on this day, in the ICU at a Manhattan hospital, my strength was tested, and a new trauma stretched my faith.

My brother's chest rises and lowers slowly. His hands are warm. He looks like he's sleeping. As soon as he wakes up, I'll surprise him with an a cappella rendition of "Happy Birthday!" Wishful thinking. It's almost 8 PM now, and we should be at the pub having a beer and singing karaoke — his go-to song is anything by Frank Sinatra. Mine is "Black Velvet" by Alannah Myles. But it's not looking like we'll make it out tonight.

The next morning, my little sister arrived from Detroit, and we spend two days at our brother's side. He doesn't wake up. During his sudden heart valve failure, he experienced extreme oxygen deprivation, and now his brain is dead. The surgeon explains that his death couldn't have been helped. This feels unimaginable. Only a few days ago, I threw him a birthday party. Then he felt a little unwell on the morning of his birthday, so I went to check on him casually. I never expected him to open the door and collapse in my arms. He was minutes away from dying alone in his apartment. But he didn't die alone; I was with him. We made it to the hospital before he died, and because of that, they were able to harvest his organs and "help countless people."

I know grief, but it's my first time losing a sibling. Losing Mom in the 90s was gut-wrenching, but her choices left us in a near-constant state of little optimism. My brother's sudden passing is different. He's a comedian and a gentle soul with a fierce desire to protect the underdog and love the unloved. He learned that from our mom.

I needed air, so I found a private place outside, away from the revolving doors and people. With a handful of tissues, I'm fully prepared to break down. But I don't break down. Instead, when I close my eyes, I see

Mom holding my little brother in her arms — they both look so peaceful. The vision of their divine togetherness brings me immeasurable peace. I feel gratitude for the opportunity to be with my brother in his final moments. I'm grateful that his life and death were not in vain. Me, in my living, and my brother, in his dying, saved lives. Once again, trauma is being used for good.

My mom gave me a beautiful gift. I feel immeasurable gratitude for the unintended lessons she taught me — resilience, acceptance, perspective, perseverance, humility, and grace, to name a few. I thank God for a broken example, a generational cycle to heal, and the words to rewrite our story. It's because of a junkie — a woman the world might consider a throwaway person — I've found uncommon strength in my life. I'm grateful for her life and death, not despite her addiction but because of it. Choosing to overcome generational pain is possible. Transcendence through trauma is achievable. The generational stronghold of my family's pain and suffering doesn't need to define my future. It ends with me. And a new chapter of love and light begins.

Marcia Dawood

marciadawood.com
Angel Investor | Thought Leader | TedX Speaker | Author

https://www.linkedin.com/in/marciadawood/
https://www.facebook.com/marcia.dawood
https://www.instagram.com/marciadawood/
www.marciadawood.com

Following an award-winning career in sales, marketing, and operations for a large education provider, Marcia Dawood now works on making people's entrepreneurial dreams come true.

She currently serves as the Chair of the Board of the Angel Capital Association - the professional society for angel investors in the United States.

Marcia is an individual investor, a Venture Partner with Mindshift Capital, an investment committee member for Next Wave Impact, and a member of Golden Seeds (one of the largest US angel groups).

Mindshift and Golden Seeds focus on investing in women-led companies. According to Bloomberg, less than 3% of early-stage investing dollars went to women in 2021. We need to change this!!!

Marcia received an MBA from UNC's Kenan-Flagler School of Business. She recently spoke at TEDx Charlotte.

She is a stepmom to 3 sons. She enjoys yoga, hiking and a nice glass of Cab Franc with her husband.

DON'T LEAVE THE ROOM EARLY BALANCING DETAILS AND EMOTIONS TO CREATE YOUR FAIRYTALE

By Marcia Dawood

My relationship started with a lie. Surprisingly, it ended up being my most truthful one. It began by committing not to leave the room early.

Have you ever felt like you are communicating, only to find out you're not being heard? Perhaps this is due to focusing on details rather than emotions. Three of my most important relationships taught me to focus on what matters most.

From a young age, I dreamed of experiencing true love—the kind of love that tugs at the heartstrings, reminiscent of fairytales and movie scenes. However, finding love is challenging, and keeping it and making it meaningful is something even Cinderella never talked about!

In my early twenties, dating was fun, but fast forward, and now in my thirties, I find myself divorced and wondering how I got there. I hoped that marriage would bring me the happiness and love I longed for, but that was not the case.

My first husband was Jewish, and I was not. We naively believed that our love would triumph over religious differences. However, this was an uphill task. Even after taking many Judaism classes and converting, his family still wouldn't accept me.

It was a challenging time for both of us, and I found it hard to articulate my feelings of rejection, sadness, and frustration. Our conversations often centered around details rather than how we felt and the toll it took on our relationship.

The conversations leading up to the wedding went like this. I would say, "Maybe I should take more classes," or, "What if we got an Orthodox rabbi to marry us?" And what I was really feeling and could have said was, "Your parents don't even know me, and this feels like I'm checking boxes to make them like me, but they have no idea who I am." But the details kept piling on. The conversations would continue with my fiancé saying, "If we kept a kosher home, two sets of dishes, two dishwashers, maybe my family would be more accepting." And what he was likely feeling was, "I don't know how to handle this situation, and because it is my family, I feel responsible for the way you must be feeling. However, I need to support them because they are my family." It was a vicious cycle.

All this was foreign to both of us and in the end, we grew apart faster than we could hold our relationship together. Our communication journey was short-sighted, and our relationship paid the price. We did not have a fairytale ending, and people were genuinely shocked when we announced our split.

I often held back from expressing my true feelings during our relationship because I didn't want to 'rock the boat.' This was not my usual personality, but I was afraid of his judgement and being vulnerable. I was afraid of the relationship ending, ending up alone, or worse, what people would say and think of me.

In hindsight, we both struggled to create a safe space to express our true feelings. We needed a level of trust to speak openly and know the other person was receptive. Neither of us was a "bad spouse," but we failed to communicate effectively about the topics that mattered most.

During my years as a divorcee, I ended up meeting several people through online dating, but it wasn't online dating that led me to my current husband. It was the good old-fashioned 'met at a bar' story. It's early in the evening, and I'm drinking water. I'm sure he only started talking to me to poke fun at me. Since he believed, at that moment, he would only see me for the next *hour* or so, he tells me, "I'm divorced with no kids." And that is where *our* communication journey begins. As I discover, there's not much truth in his statement.

Over the next few weeks, the entire '747 airplane full of baggage' is revealed to me as our relationship develops—definitely not a horse and carriage size. I catch the end of a conversation he was having on the phone that sounded like he was talking to children. Curious, I ask who he was talking to, and after some roundabout excuses he finally admits he has three sons—all under ten. I'm thinking, "Whoa . . . this is a big deal! Three kids?!? Three little kids?!?" I need a few minutes to process this new information, but now I am starting to question every conversation we've had up until now.

He says, "I'm sorry I lied, but I wasn't sure how to tell you the truth. The timing just never seemed right." He adds, "I'm sure you don't want to see me again." And I'm thinking, "Wait a minute. I'm still processing what I'm learning. People don't usually lie without a reason, and there has to be more to the story." He repeats himself at least three more times, something like "I'm sure you don't want to see me again" and then, "This is over."

The only way I could get him to stop saying this and talk to me was for me to blurt out, "I'm not leaving! Sit down, and we will discuss this, but *no one is leaving.*" Suddenly the air became a little lighter, and the tension eased a bit. Not leaving the room made him let go of the assumption that *I* was leaving. A commitment was made, and without realizing it, I created a safe space to talk without worrying the other person would run out.

At that moment, I was talking about leaving the room, but this approach can be effective when applied to leaving of any kind. Leaving the room, the building, the state, the relationship, or even more subtle but profound, the conversation. Changing the subject can be a strong avoidance tactic that can leave the others in the conversation feeling like the 'subject changer' left the room physically.

Now that expectations were set and a relatively safe space was created, I said, "Are there any other big life circumstances you would like to tell me?" Of course, I'm thinking, what could be more significant than having three children I didn't know about? But I can tell by his look that there's more.

I tell him, "The only way this is going to work is if you tell me everything, the whole truth." He hesitates, not because he doesn't want to tell me the truth, but because he thinks, at what point will my life look too complicated for her to stay? I finally say, "I'm still sitting here after you told me part of this, you might as well tell me the rest, but if you leave anything out now when you have this unique opportunity, the trust between us will likely be beyond repair."

He needed this invitation to let down his guard and explain more of the details he had left out. I knew his ex-wife lived in a different city, far enough that getting there required a plane ride, and now I knew children were living there too. He explains he had committed to visitation with the kids every third weekend. And, in his separation agreement, which wasn't *completely* finalized yet, he committed to a level of support beyond the legal requirements. At this point, I'm starting to understand that his financial situation is strained. And then he adds that he also financially supports his parents, who live in another country.

"Anything else?" I ask as I'm trying to process all this information. "No. I understand if this is too much for you to sign up for." The easy road here would have been to run—not walk—in the other direction, especially since we had only seen each other for a few weeks. But having to talk about significant life issues so early in our relationship helped us communicate better on many levels. Sure, no one likes being lied to, but the way the truth came out became our best communication method. And what we were really talking about was a commitment to each other and to staying in the room.

Since, in the beginning, I didn't run at the first sign of conflict, he developed a level of trust in me that still, to this day, many years later, continues to grow. And yes, there were a lot of details to work through over the twelve or so years as the kids grew up. When details and logistics started to take over and emotions began running high, we committed to talking through the feelings as much as the details.

If I'm making it sound easy, it wasn't. Life is messy and complicated. We certainly did not have just one or two conversations before everything was fine. We had many, many conversations, and during those, we always followed these guidelines:

- We commit to one another, and no one leaves the room during the conversation. This helps build the trust needed to talk about hard things and be open to hearing the truth.

- We agree to be open to inviting a conversation that includes challenging issues and feelings. This can be one of the most difficult steps. A little like when you know you need to work out, and just putting on your gym clothes and showing up at the gym is a huge step. Once you are there, the workout is easy. It's getting there that can be the hardest part.

- We agree about what we are about to discuss. We can't solve every issue in one conversation. "Rome wasn't built in a day," as the saying goes, and it's true that not all issues can be solved at once. Determining the most important topic that needs discussion helps all involved to know the agenda and feel comfortable sticking to it.

- We promise to reflect honestly on what the other person said.

At the end of the conversation, summarize what your partner said and have your partner summarize what you said. That exercise helps everyone feel heard.

All three boys are now in college, and while traveling to see them every third weekend for over twelve years was a huge commitment, it was worth it. They got to have a strong relationship with their dad, and they know they are loved and cared about. And along the way, I got to be a step-mom to three amazing humans. And my second marriage is its own version of a fairytale. My husband and I are best friends and more in love every day.

Romantic relationships aren't the only ones needing open and honest communication. In 2016, my mother was diagnosed with ALS, also known as Lou Gehrig's disease, and passed away in April 2018. ALS is a debilitating neurological disorder that progressively impairs the body's muscles, starting with the inability to walk or talk and eventually leading to an inability to breathe.

My mom was understandably frightened and overwhelmed by the rapid progression of her illness, and she withdrew emotionally from me and my dad, her spouse of over 50 years. Despite my efforts to talk with her and offer emotional support, she became so upset that I felt forced to change the subject in an attempt to avoid causing her any further distress.

One day, I asked her who gave her the crystal bowl in the dining room. She knew I was asking because there wasn't much time left. She immediately started to cry, so I reacted quickly by changing the subject. I knew she was in so much emotional pain due to the diagnosis, and I didn't want to cause any more pain.

She was insistent that only my dad and I could take care of her, refusing outside assistance, which added to the stress of her care. As a result, the details of her care became our sole focus. Bathing was one of the hardest. Her disease was progressing so fast. It started with her not being able to stand anymore in the shower, so we got a shower stool. But then getting her in and out of the shower was hard. Each change to the shower routine due to her lack of mobility brought on a whole new level of anxiety.

In hindsight, I wish I had talked with her more about what she needed emotionally—to feel safe and supported during her illness. Maybe if she had felt comfortable expressing her emotions, it may have helped her process her feelings, and we could have offered her more meaningful support during her final days. I wish I had gotten her, my dad, and I to agree to discuss how each of us was feeling "without leaving the room" and without changing the subject to something lighter.

Looking back, I remember a few times we would start to talk about emotions, and one of us got uncomfortable and changed the subject, usually by going back to focusing on the details and logistics of her care. Yes, she died knowing that we loved her, but without ever talking about her life, her legacy, or how much we knew she loved us.

Reflecting on these three relationships, I realize how important effective communication of emotions and details can be to building and maintaining a healthy relationship. Yet, creating that kind of communication is easy to say, yet hard to execute. No one is perfect, and we need to have grace with ourselves and each other in all types of relationships.

As I continue to grow and learn, I have become more intentional about how I spend my time and who I spend it with. I seek out positive people who are supportive and uplift me. Doing so allows me to recognize certain friendships or relationships that no longer serve me, and I can consciously decide to let them go. I find more joy in building friendships and relationships based on open communication where everyone is willing to share their true feelings and be vulnerable. That vulnerability helps us all grow.

Incorporating healthy communication into all aspects of my life has been transformative. I did find my Prince Charming, even though he wasn't alone on the horse he rode in on.

Every woman has her own journey. We create our own fairytales. The most enchanting ones are not left to fate, but built on a commitment to ourselves and the ones we love.

Vera Milan Gervais

VMG Unlimited
Speaker | Mindset Mentor | Creating Confidence with
Wordz We Wear®

https://www.linkedin.com/in/vera-milan-gervais-652a42b/
https://www.facebook.com/vera.milan.gervais
https://www.instagram.com/vera_milan_gervais/
https://www.veragervais.com/

Vera Milan Gervais is an author, speaker, award-winning businesswoman and mindset mentor who helps women develop confidence and show up with presence. Her signature Wordz We Wear® program explores how word labels – the words we use to talk to and about ourselves – are like clothing labels. They influence who we are and who we can become.

Vera's health history and experiences as an entrepreneur, writer, marketer, and strategic consultant shaped her perspective on success and well-being. A birth defect resulted in four major surgeries before she turned 18 and left her with a leg length difference, scoliosis and osteoarthritis. Yet she's an avid hiker, gardener and photographer who has climbed mountains, built several businesses with her husband, and explored all seven continents with her family!

The mother of two talented and amazing young adults, Vera lives near the ocean in New Brunswick, Canada with her husband and business partner, Marcel.

A ROSE IS JUST A ROSE

By Vera Milan Gervais

I don't understand why I can't give you red roses because of something that happened before I even met you.

It was our 25th wedding anniversary. My husband and I were sipping wine and watching fireworks through the arched window of our elegant villa in Italy. A creeping vine clung to the window frame, and the scent of its roses drifted in with the evening breeze. Except for the presence of roses, it was a perfect celebration of our love.

Red roses were my nemesis. They triggered a physical and emotional reaction that, at minimum, made me restless. At worst, they left me in cold sweats. It doesn't sound rational, but it was real. A rose could reduce me to tears in seconds.

My husband knew the story. He knew why I didn't like red roses. He knew I loved him and adored our life together. But it was obvious something about my rose paranoia hurt him. It was as if a thorn from my past was embedded in our marriage and resulted in a festering sore—as if the past wasn't really in the past.

In a sense, it wasn't. When I was in my twenties, I was stalked by roses. Red roses would show up on my doorstep, at my office, or even on the hood of my car whenever a new boyfriend entered my life. Even without a signed card, I knew who they were from.

Red roses meant an abusive ex was watching me and wanted me to know it. I moved to a different province, but he found me. I repeatedly moved apartments. The roses followed. As long as I stayed single and silent, there were no roses. As soon as I started living and hoping, roses showed up to remind me I didn't deserve happiness.

Your lot in life is suffering.

That message was ingrained in me since childhood. I was born with a physical handicap which, in addition to constant pain and endless surgeries, made me the brunt of teasing and bullying. At times I welcomed the physical pain raging through my back and legs. When my nerves were preoccupied with coping, my brain didn't have the capacity to criticize and condemn me. Pain blocked the nasty voices lurking in the corners of my mind—the ones whispering that I was defective and would never be worthy of love.

Sadly, I accepted my fate. I was brought up in an Irish Catholic household with the litany that suffering on earth is rewarded in the afterlife. Since I lived with constant pain, seeing any merit in suffering allowed me to keep my head down and pretend I was okay.

But the question my husband quietly asked on one of the happiest days of our lives forced me to think about the past. His simple question made me aware that I'd allowed shame and guilt to control my life for over 30 years. I'd lived in the shadows, never daring to take the stage or write a book because I didn't want to be in the limelight.

I'd lived in fear that a rose would land at my feet and destroy my happiness.

How could this fear still control me? Decades had passed since roses taunted me. I was married to an incredibly optimistic man who made me laugh and gave me the freedom to grow. And at the same time, he held me close and made me feel safe. We built a successful business together. We traveled the world with our children. We bought and renovated property. Life was stimulating and rewarding.

So why couldn't I let go of my past? Why was it still possible for red roses to trigger a sense of fear and unworthiness in me? They were just flowers. Yet seeing or smelling them could elicit a physical reaction, especially when it was unexpected. I once started shaking so badly when an early Valentine's Day display surprised me that I left the store without my purchases.

When I finally decided to explore my negative attachment to red roses, I was surprised at how intensely my mind and body resisted. Every time I started to reflect, I created a diversion. I was afraid to dig deep and ruin my life. I was afraid of falling apart.

I might have continued to deny this foreboding forever, but my husband had trusted our love enough to mention his pain. It was up to me to deal with mine.

I bought a red rose and put it in a vase in my *zen* room. It's the room I retreat to when I want calm and balance. The room where I meditate, do yoga, write morning pages, journal, and dream. The room where I've always felt safe.

Bringing a rose into my safe space was like bringing a rabid animal into my home. I shrunk into the creases of an oversized chair, my journal in hand, its blank page glaringly white under the lamplight. My calm was shattered. I'd opened a door I could never close again.

You're stupid. You're ugly. You're crippled. You're useless. You're worthless.

The voices screamed relentlessly. They had never been silent, but I'd muted them by constantly filling my brain and my time with work, writing, and activities. Nagging whispers had taunted me for decades, but I could ignore them as long as I avoided thinking about the past. And as long as I avoided roses.

Bringing a rose into my sanctuary set off alarms. The careful calm I'd cultivated when I met and married Marcel, when our two terrific children were born, and when we'd built our businesses, our home, our life, and our incredible love... that calm was withering around the edges, turning brown, trembling, and dropping along with the petals from the dying rose on my table.

Young Vera, the badgered young girl who had fled the roses, had never escaped. She'd hidden her pain, covered her scars, and stayed silent all those years. Now she was reaching out, searching for love. I couldn't ignore her.

I started to write to this sad and scared girl. My morning pages became a mishmash of memories, excuses, apologies, questions, and fear. I cried. I screamed. I scratched huge Xs across pages. I tore an entire notebook into tiny pieces.

I was afraid of the dark places she and I shared. Yet I knew whatever was keeping me hiding from myself, was also keeping me from becoming my best self.

And I knew I needed help. I reached out to dear friends who had known me throughout my crazy journey, grateful for their presence. They encouraged me to celebrate how far I had come and let go of what I couldn't change. Their support helped me continue showing up and functioning, but I wasn't healing.

I kept lashing out at my younger self. I couldn't understand how she could be so intelligent and yet so stupid at the same time. She had not only walked into a bad relationship, she'd stayed in it too long. All because she hadn't wanted to admit she'd made a mistake. Again.

Even as I was trying to free this naive young part of me from her suffering, I was belittling her with criticism and condemnation. I couldn't forgive her.

My breakthrough came at a facilitated Brene Brown *Daring Way* weekend retreat. For those who don't know this work, it's about worthiness. The weekend was an emotional rollercoaster, but I left with one clear insight: the darkness I feared wasn't about a man or a rose. It was about me not loving myself.

I'd allowed a mistake to define me. Instead of learning from a bad choice, I had chained it around my heart and let it drag me down whenever I tried to fly. I'd attached a sense of unworthiness to my soul identity.

The wonderful women at the retreat helped me make a resolution that weekend. My therapy would be to do what I do well—write. I committed to writing about *The Rose*. As I filled the pages with fears and facts, what started as detailing my memories became a novel.

I outlined the events I remembered from those painful years, and I let them talk to me. I didn't know how many were true or how many were distorted. Over the intervening years, how many of my *memories* had been convoluted by tales from books, movies, music, and other women's stories?

I wasn't sure. But I knew I couldn't heal until I surrendered to the fear of finding out.

Surrendering meant capturing my worst nightmares on the page. I started by documenting my flawed memories and then embroidered them by weaving in events that may never have happened. I drew on the stories other women told me about controlling and abusive men in their lives. I added details from books I'd read. I poured it all onto the page and turned my trauma into a drama. After a while, I lost track of which parts were real and which were fiction. Somehow, dragging my memories into the light and taking my experiences to the nth degree took the terror out of them.

Memories are stories we tell ourselves, and stories change in the telling.

I realized I could write this fictional story however I wanted, which also meant I could interpret it differently. I gave the story a happy ending. I gave the young woman back her identity. It was a tenuous and emotional acceptance; I was letting go of something that was no longer relevant or important to my life.

As a step towards clearing the emotional debris, I attempted to publish the novel. The timing wasn't optimal, as the pandemic hit and every published author was writing another book. Even though it was a bad time for a new author, I promised a friend I would get 15 rejections from agents before throwing in the towel. When I reached 15, she suggested I try another 15 submissions.

With a strange sense of calm, I realized I didn't have to. Writing the novel had been a gift to myself. It allowed me to release the demons holding me back all those years. I shelved the book and instead bought myself a dozen red roses.

Sometimes it's difficult to figure out what's holding us back from fully expressing who we are and what we are capable of. In my case, whenever I saw a red rose, it triggered a sense of worthlessness and a fear of never being lovable.

I'd allowed a red rose, the symbol of love, to eat away at my *self* love. Roses reminded me of the unwitting mistakes I'd made in my early 20s and how those mistakes labeled me as a failure. I'd never dealt with the fear and pain of those years, which permitted my inner voices to keep taunting me, and left me doubting my worthiness.

Despite how beautifully my life had turned around, negativity had survived in my subconscious mind for over 30 years. I was in a loving relationship. I had two exceptional children, a solid career, and a life I loved.

Yet a red rose could completely unravel my self-esteem.

I learned from some of the research I did for my novel that our brains don't have filters for truth and fiction. When we tell ourselves stories, our brains believe them. All those stories I'd told myself over the years had solidified into beliefs that became my truths—even though they may have been tainted by time.

I do have some clear memories. A man had been physical with me and had wanted to control me. He made sure I knew he was following me, and yes, that scared me. And because that demeaning relationship occurred shortly after my first marriage ended, I assumed I wasn't worthy of real love.

The combination led me to doubt my ability to judge people and destroyed my self-esteem. I withdrew into silence, even abandoning friendships, because I was convinced they'd find out how stupid I was and I'd be rejected again.

Taking time to document and assess my muddy memories gave me both release and awareness. I finally understood that I hadn't spent all those years hiding because of *what* happened, but rather because I believed I had invited the abuse. I was too young and naive to know I was being manipulated by someone else telling me who I was.

I filed the novel in my archives and celebrated with a rose tattoo on my leg. When the young lady who inked the tattoo asked me what the rose symbolized, I said: *Freedom.* She was surprised. Apparently, most people tell her *love.*

And she's partly right.

The rose tattoo proclaims that I have given myself permission to love fully. To love myself, my husband, and my life. After all, a red rose is a symbol of love.

But a rose is just a rose. Knowing I deserve love is what has given me the freedom to love unconditionally.

Sue Bevan Baggott

Power Within Consulting, LLC
Speaker | Author | Innovator | Angel Investor | Executive Advisor

https://www.linkedin.com/in/suebaggott1/
https://www.facebook.com/sbbaggott
https://www.secure.instagram.com/sue.baggott/
www.powerwithinconsulting.com
www.suebevanbaggott.com

Over her career journey from Global Innovation Leader at Procter & Gamble (growing mega-brands from Pantene to Pampers) to Founder of Power Within Consulting to "Accidental" Angel Investor and Startup Advisor, Sue Bevan Baggott discovered the superpower of empathetic human connections to drive more meaningful leadership, innovation, and entrepreneurial success.

Sue's mission is to empower positive impact through innovation and connection. She strives to drive important change in our world through her speaking, writing, consulting, coaching, angel investing, and board roles - all in collaboration with purpose-driven leaders and organizations.

Investing to accelerate positive change, Sue's portfolio of early-stage companies spans funds with Next Wave Impact, Queen City Angels, Mindshift Capital, and more.

Happily married for 30+ years to Steve, her supportive husband, Sue enjoys reading, travel, nature, art, theater, and sharing time with family and friends. She's the loving mother of Alex Baggott-Rowe, his wife Allison, and Chris Baggott.

BREAK THROUGH LIMITING BELIEFS TO UNLEASH POWER WITHIN

By Sue Bevan Baggott

My Scariest Night

I awaken to the sound of sobbing from our living room. Scared but curious, I tiptoe down the stairs of our tiny suburban home to find out what was going on.

As I descend, I see my mother crumpled on our living room floor as my dad tries to console her. In my ten years of childhood, I've seen my caring, sensitive mom cry before, but nothing as out of control as this.

I love my mom, so I feel a powerful desire to help, but we are powerless to calm her.

My dad calls for emergency responders to assist in taking mom to the hospital psych ward. As they depart, dad asks me to keep watch over my two younger sisters still sleeping upstairs.

That night's experience ignited my drive to do everything possible to help our family during mom's battles with the highs and lows of her unpredictable mental illness.

In the early 1970s, when mom experienced her first breakdown, mental illness was highly misunderstood and severely stigmatized. Families often hid emotional struggles out of fear or embarrassment.

Our family endured rocky times. We felt like walking a tightrope in a windstorm trying to navigate mom's unpredictable mood shifts and avoid setting off emotional outbursts. Sadly, it took years before doctors and therapists could provide mom with more extended periods of emotional stability.

counseling to help me understand my mom's illness and know I was not to blame.

Personally, I had to grow up fast and take on a lot of extra responsibilities caring for my sisters when my dad escaped into his work and my mom was struggling. When my mom's bipolar disorder created an unpredictable roller-coaster of emotions in our home, I tried to gain control by focusing on succeeding at school.

Prior to mom's breakdown, I was a bright, outgoing student whom teachers and other students liked. After mom's breakdown, I overcompensated by becoming a perfectionist with a strong drive for academic achievement and a high level of intolerance for my missteps. Unfortunately, I teared up easily when I made mistakes in class, which made me a target of frequent bullying for being a "smarty pants" and "cry-baby." These were painful labels that hurt my feelings and limited my friendships. Add in being teased about my frugal, home-sewn clothing and "shrimp" stature. As a pre-teen and teenager yearning to fit in socially, it was embarrassing to stand out for all the wrong reasons.

Since mental health challenges were taboo, I was ashamed to share my mom's struggles with anyone outside our immediate family. While I desperately wanted to be accepted, I hesitated to let others visit our home or get too close.

Fortunately, in contrast to some of the negative voices I encountered, I also had some very positive influences in my life.

Eventually, I found a few equally nerdy yet empathetic friends with whom I could share the truth about my mom's bipolar battles and my personal struggles. Those friends supported me through junior high, high school, and beyond. Decades later, I remain close to these long-time special friends.

My paternal grandfather was also a significant positive influence. I loved spending time together during summer visits to Virginia Beach or meeting for Lehigh football games. His encouraging advice: "Use your talents to their fullest in service of others," still guides me today.

Grandad Bevan was a man ahead of his time in seeing beyond stereotypes. From an early age, he told me: "Girls can be anything they want to be." He genuinely believed that girls and women could be or do anything men could. He supported my interests in science and math and encouraged me to pursue engineering. He told me, "Engineers learn to solve tough problems and make the world a better place."

As my biggest cheerleader, mentor, and role model, Grandad Bevan was exceptionally proud when I decided to study Chemical Engineering and Biology at his alma mater, Lehigh University. With a 10:1 ratio of men to women in my engineering classes, my college experiences taught me a lot about collaborating and succeeding in a male-dominated environment. Gratefully, my grandfather lived long enough to see me graduate from Lehigh, and he was proud when I began my global innovation career at Procter & Gamble.

Challenges Lead to Valuable Lessons

Despite our tensions and misunderstandings, I now recognize that my parents tried to do their best with the resources and perspectives they had at the time. Today, I'm grateful to have invested time and effort in communications to bridge our differences and build positive, loving relationships with my father and mother.

As a couple, my parents experienced many ups and downs, but I admire them for keeping their marriage together through love, faith, counseling, and commitment. I'm grateful for my dad's many positive traits, including loyally supporting my mother through her mental health challenges, something not all men would have done. Plus, I appreciate my mother's caring nature, encouraging my love of reading, and being courageous in managing her bipolar disorder.

My combined childhood challenges taught me many valuable lessons about breaking through limiting beliefs to access and unleash my power.

Trying to prove I could do anything boys could do, plus navigating my mom's bipolar disorder, taught me that gritty persistence—physically and emotionally—could overcome most obstacles.

With strong aspirations, determination, and incremental steps over time, I overcame childhood asthma. I built significant endurance and strength and achieved meaningful athletic goals—even if I couldn't become a son. Learning to love sports gave me better health alongside wonderful leadership, coaching, and team collaboration experiences that have served me well.

Learning the power of empathetic human connection and resilience during my mom's struggles with mental illness helped me build emotional intelligence. Today, I recognize that my emotional sensitivity not only enabled me to foster strong personal relationships, but it's also a valuable asset in driving my professional success as a human-centered innovator and leader.

Accessing Power Within

I think we all face times when people question our capabilities, choices, motivations, or commitments, and these negative voices can lead to us question ourselves. We must not let these naysayers diminish us, but instead, turn their doubts into our fuel to prove them wrong.

To grow and move forward, we must refuse to be underestimated and focus on cultivating positive, encouraging, supportive voices to listen to. Those that lift us up during difficult times and give us hope.

Maybe you've had family members, friends, teachers, mentors, or bosses who saw your potential and believed in you.

- Keep their encouragement front and center.

- When you encounter doubters or under-estimators—where you've had to work hard to prove yourself…

- Hold on to the power of determination and grit you may have gained.

- But let go of the voices saying you can't measure up (even if they come from within).

Mastering a mindset that ensures positive forces outweigh negative forces is the key to meaningful success in life. Accessing the power within us can enable us to achieve almost anything. With the right mindset, encouraging supporters, willingness to grow and learn, along with gritty determination, we can accomplish more than we realize.

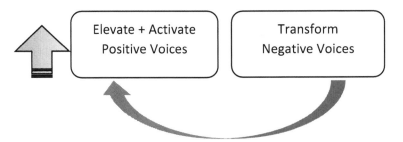

Elevate + Activate Positive Voices	Transform Negative Voices
• Seek out and listen to the voices of people who recognize your talents, believe in you, and encourage you. • Cultivate encouraging voices to stretch you and help you achieve goals you may not have thought possible.	• Turn under-estimators' doubts into fuel to drive you forward. • Stop spending time with those who fail to recognize your talents or try to dim your light. • Don't allow negative voices to hold you back from your goals or dreams.

Remember that you have unique gifts—even superpowers—that you are meant to bring to our world, so please don't hold yourself back. I have confidence that you can develop empathetic connections and communications to enhance all the relationships in your life. Plus, you can build the physical and/or mental strength required to achieve meaningful goals by following these ABCs:

- Aspire – to achieve your dreams.
- Believe – in your inner superpowers and in your ability to grow your gritty persistence through trial, failure, and learning.
- Connect Courageously – to leverage the power of empathetic human connections and gain support from others, including professional support, if you or someone close to you shows signs of mental health challenges.

Recognize that you also have incredible power to help others achieve their goals. Be the positive, empowering force in the lives of those who might be underestimated.

My mission is to empower positive impact through innovation and connection. In sharing my story and lessons, I hope to empower you to break through any limiting beliefs you encounter so you can also access your superpowers to achieve your goals and aspirations.

Allison Baggott-Rowe

Author | Speaker | Teacher

https://www.linkedin.com/in/allison-baggott-rowe-2226356a/
https://www.facebook.com/allison.a.baggottrowe
https://www.instagram.com/allison.baggottrowe/
https://allisonbaggottrowe.com/

Award-winning author and TEDx speaker, Allison Baggott-Rowe is a graduate student pursuing her ALM in Creative Writing and Literature at Harvard Extension School. She earned her M.A. in Psychology from Xavier University where her research focused on mindfulness and strengths-based goal setting. She teaches creative writing to people of all ages through virtual workshops and in the classroom. Allison has a wealth of creative experiences including performing as an aerialist, earning a title as one of the Top 100 Female Chess players in the United States, and receiving national medals for excellence in Irish Music performance as well as the Swarthmore Book Award. When she is not writing from her favorite perch on the couch, Allison spends her time with family and friends, taking her dogs (Samwise and Rosie) to the park, and embarking on adventures with her husband, Alex, into the wilds of Ohio or playing enchanting tabletop boardgames.

SERENITY

By Allison Baggott-Rowe

The last time I saw my father alive, he was jumpstarting my car. Standing in the stillness of that November night, I watched as his hands connected the heart of his Ford Mustang to my Toyota Highlander. He grinned as the engine roared to life, though moments before we'd wondered if this was the end for my beloved car. It had been in my family for many years before coming during college to me. To transfer the car into my name, my father sold me the Highlander for exactly $1. I was grateful as his worn, weathered hands accepted the crumpled bill from mine.

"Love you, angel," he said. His quick fingers smoothed the dollar straight before tucking it into his wallet behind the family photos, sequestered from the bills of lesser sentimental value. He handed me the keys as I embraced him.

"I love you, too."

Growing up, my father had spent countless hours under the hood of that car showing me where certain parts were housed. How they functioned. How they might malfunction. He knew that I had no particular interest in cars, and really, neither did he. The practice came about after I suffered an anxiety attack that no medication could relax. My father decided to try something new and untested. So began my lessons learning about the car we nicknamed after the spaceship in one of our favorite sci-fi shows. We called her "Serenity."

I couldn't help but identify with Serenity. Something new was always changing the way she operated. She was forced to adapt again and again. Sort of like me.

The first time someone told me I would have a "new normal" was when I was diagnosed with type 1 diabetes at age six. The next was just a few months later with a subsequent diagnosis of severe anxiety as I learned to manage the life-threatening disease at such a tender age. A "new normal" is never good. It's a phrase reserved for illness, loss, and periods of painful growth. Over my abbreviated childhood and teen years, I found myself faced with an onslaught of "new normals" as I was diagnosed with more than ten autoimmune disorders. As my dad and I crammed our bags for father-daughter backpacking trips, I couldn't help but notice the mounting medical supplies weighing down our once-unburdened packs. There was no room for anything frivolous if I wanted to stay safe.

An instinctual binary evolved, and I began to compartmentalize the world around me into "rights" and "wrongs." Were my blood sugars good or bad? High or low? Safe or deadly? Anger, fear, and guilt slipped into my subconscious as silent interlopers, weaving seamlessly into the dark composite of my shadow everywhere I went. Every new bend in the road brought the expectation of a new diagnosis lurking just out of sight, but right around the corner. A bogeyman that lived in my bones.

Day after day, my father drove me to the same high school he attended. On the mornings I was too ill to go to school, he swaddled me in blankets on the living room sofa and kissed me on the forehead. The days I was well enough to attend classes, he let me choose the music as he piloted Serenity down the highway. The CD player alternated between a blast of Irish jigs, reels, and sea shanties, and melancholy musicals that left us both in tears. *Les Mis* was a mutual favorite. Dad cranked the radio loud, and I loved him for it.

We sang together at the top of our lungs before pulling up to the drop-off circle. From there, Dad would either see me off with a wave or unpack the wheelchair I intermittently required. He would wheel me to class, still singing, as I hid my face in embarrassment. Despite the challenges of finishing high school with (mostly) invisible disabilities,

I did graduate. To my doctors' amazement, I went on to college, though we limited my applications to colleges a five-hour drive from my parents. Both would make frequent trips to help manage flare-ups of my disabilities as well as a traumatic brain injury (TBI) when I was assaulted in my second year of college.

My head was slammed in a door seven times before first responders rushed me to the hospital. Though I was battered and beaten up, I refused to be flat-out beaten. In hindsight, I'm glad I didn't know then the attack would be the first of two assaults I would survive.

Both my mother and father supported my transfer from Oberlin College, where my sense of self and safety had eroded in the wake of the TBI, to The Ohio State University. I was welcomed into both the Honors program and an outpatient rehabilitation program to help me regain the function I lost from my TBI. I relearned the basics of walking, talking, and existing in a world that continued to prove itself both frightening and magical. After 1,408 days, I passed the post-concussive protocol and went out with friends to celebrate the milestone.

At the time, I had just started seeing someone new. It wasn't serious, just something casual...or so I thought before being sexually assaulted when we returned to my apartment after the celebration. All the self-doubt I had experienced as a child with autoimmune issues and then as an adult recovering from a TBI came flooding back in the wake of surviving this second assault from a different assailant. How much could one body take?

Time passed.

I thought I could leave that night behind me. Put it in a box under the stairs labeled "do not open." But that is not how boxes work. Or trauma, as it turns out. I compartmentalized my hurts and tried half-heartedly to convince myself what had happened was not my fault. But my semblance of serenity was shattered.

Several months later, we took a family vacation to a beach in Florida. The first morning, I rose before my mother and brother awoke. My loneliness was more palpable in the presence of my loving family, whom I had avoided up until now. I was supposed to be having fun, but my shameful secret had grown too large to manage on my own. I had not told anyone after quietly pursuing emergency services in the immediate aftermath, alone. Shuffling into the living room, I sat opposite my father for a long moment.

With a blistered heart, I told the first man who had ever loved me what I had done. What had been done to me. He remained one of the few to know—until now. I never meant to break my father's heart, though I knew that's exactly what I was doing as I found the courage to finally confess that I had been the victim of sexual assault, a wrinkle in the fabric of my soul that no amount of ironing could press straight again. Or so I thought until he hugged me.

I looked into the kind, cerulean eyes of a man who had always smelled of coffee, sweat, and safety. Though I was now in my early twenties, my father patted his knee for me to sit just above his 10-inch scar. I had always admired that scar, a remnant of an old volleyball injury. I looked at the white line emblazoned on his already tan skin. *Such strength,* my younger self had thought. *My father has faced the world head-on and still went back for more. What could be braver? What could be realer?*

Scars are the only tattoos we really earn.

Keenly aware of my pounding heart, I felt the fragments of my heart clash together and scrape the hollowness inside my chest as I lowered myself into his lap. Dad was in his swim trunks and one of those Hawaiian shirts that made me start humming the Beach Boys involuntarily. His arms wound around my waist, and for the first time in several months, I allowed the tears to slip from my eyes as he cradled the pieces of me together while we watched the sun come up.

For a long time, I didn't talk about the assault again. But I thought about it daily. When I went running, I was ever watchful of men who might want to peel me from the path at a moment's notice. Keys poked through my fingers like Wolverine claws as I pushed a Kroger shopping cart through the grocery store parking lot. I checked and double-checked the rooms in my apartment for my rapist, who might be hiding, lying in wait for a second attempt. Though he was never there, my assailant was omnipresent.

My therapist called it "hypervigilance." I called it survival.

When I entered into my next serious relationship, I told my partner. Two weeks into the relationship. Over Skype. I was afraid if I didn't tell him straight out of the gate, I might never work up the courage in the future. I worried that not telling him would be lying to him. I believed myself to be "damaged goods," and he deserved to know what he was signing up for in a relationship with a survivor of sexual assault, though I wasn't certain myself.

I was prepared for him to say any of the number of things I had heard when bad things happened over the years. I was prepared for the subtle shift of energy as he would palpably distance himself. I was prepared to comfort him in the decision to go our separate ways.

What I was not prepared for was the silence that hung low between us through the eerie blue-light of the computer screen. The creases of skin contracting around his boyish face as he raised a hand to rub his chin. Then more silence.

"I'm so sorry," he said at length, before reaching to hug me through his laptop monitor. I wept as his T-shirt pressed against the camera lens. I leaned into the hug that spanned more than 400 miles, desperate to trust his belief in us while simultaneously bracing for the day he would choose to walk away.

But he didn't leave. Instead, we moved up our plans to visit in person. It did not take long before we fell in love. Then, we moved in together. Completely unplanned, we separately asked the others' parents for their blessing to propose to one another. We were engaged at Christmas a year and a half after that tough Skype conversation. Though medical challenges continued to crop up, we were both all in. Our families were waiting with champagne.

But when I woke one morning to find my mother sobbing on the edge of our bed, my fiancé already gone for work, I felt the blood drain from my head as though someone had cracked an egg on my scalp and reality oozed down the sides of my face. My father had suffered a fatal heart attack. Just like that, he was a memory whose phone number took me to voicemail. No more backpacking trips, or Beach Boys, or forehead kisses. My mother and I held each other, weeping for the call we had to make to my brother before so many others.

When we got the autopsy back my family was shocked to learn that this was not his first, but second heart attack. Despite reassurances that not even my father had known about the first silent heart attack, my mind reeled. I wondered how things might have been different if I had not assaulted him with the truth of what had happened to me that day in Florida and weakened a heart so big, he refused to turn anyone away. After all the emotional strain I had heaped on my father since I was a little girl with big feelings… had I killed my father?

My fiancé drove Serenity and me to the service. My brother and I delivered his eulogy at the funeral. We stood shoulder to shoulder in front of the hundreds of people who came to say goodbye to the man who had made the idea of relationships safe again for me—who had made the idea of my fiancé safe. The man who had encouraged me not to give up on loving relationships in the early hours of a morning in Florida when I had felt that all hope was lost. After we spoke about our father, my brother and I returned to our seats, flanking my mother. My fiancé squeezed my shoulder, and I felt the ephemeral tug of the divine as I stared up at the minister who delivered the final words for my father. The same minister who would marry us only six months later with no father-daughter dance. When my husband and I would dance to "Come What May."

In the couple of years after my father's death, I swam against a turbulent current of grief. It manifested as physical pain and threatened to open old wounds as fear crept back into the corners of my world. My husband's face would often shift to that of one of my two assailants, and I once ran screaming from him in the middle of the night when I woke from a nightmare.

Cocooned in layers of blankets tucked lovingly around my body, I would look up to see my husband's blue eyes smiling back at me as he brushed the hair back from my face. Over the next few months, my shoulders relaxed as he gently pulled a brush through my hair, allowing me to truly rest and process my grief. In the shelter of his acceptance, a tender part of my soul grew still and slow. That frenetic part of my ever-watchful mind fluttered and fell into a gentle rhythm, lulled by the belief that I was not only allowed to be safe and happy, but that I was *becoming* safe and happy.

Though the steps I took were not linear, my husband supported me as I began therapy with a trauma counselor. I embraced the myriad benefits of trauma therapy for C-PTSD (complex PTSD), which demystified and destigmatized all the components that make me, me. My husband proved a stalwart sentinel as I reforged connections with friends and family that had been neglected in the shadow of my own grief. I chose to return to school, this time pursuing my true passion for writing. With gentle guidance, I became ready to not only trust my husband's support but to support myself again, too.

As time moved onward, I continued to grow in the chrysalis we built together and felt the energy of my heart begin to transform. A warmth emanated from the space in my chest where I once felt shards of a misused heart tearing at the cloth of my skin to escape. Though scarred, my heart now beats in a full, rounded way, as do all hearts who have relearned to trust. I think of the scars on my father's knee and consider my own with fresh insight.

After waking up to a kaleidoscope of promising tomorrows, I reflect with self-compassion on so many bleak yesterdays. I will always live a life with disabilities, *and* it's a life worth living. None of us escape the scars and invisible injuries of life if we're living it well. But if we allow ourselves to be seen—*truly seen*—by another person, our hurts have the ability to heal. When we turn that lens inward and truly see ourselves, I believe we can find the peace and compassion that promote healing. For me, the heart of that healing will always reside in acceptance.

Accepting myself as a person with disabilities and a survivor of sexual assault has opened a door to a realer, more robust love toward myself and others. Each day I feel an immense gratitude for having found the space to trust myself again in the harbors of safe, blue eyes. Knowing Serenity is parked right outside, I am eager to continue life's bumpy journey with my husband and all the other people who help us to pilot her. Some days I still need his help to get dressed. Other days we run miles for marathon training together. But no matter how I get into my pajamas each night, the last thing I hear, say, and mean, before falling asleep is:

"I love you."

"I love you, too."

Cheryl Field, MSN, RN, CRRN

www.cherylfield.com
www.linkedin.com/in/cherylfield1621
https://www.facebook.com/cheryl.field.18

Cheryl Field has 30+ years experience in nursing, specializing in rehabilitation in the post-acute area with a focus on analytics, compliance, quality, and reimbursement. Cheryl has served a variety of roles, including clinical director, VP of Healthcare, Chief Product Officer and most recently as Group Product Leader. Cheryl has spoken at state and national conventions over 25 years on a variety of healthcare care industry topics. She makes learning complex systems easy with simple analogies, relevant and often personal stories to maximize audience engagement. Cheryl is certified in Rehabilitation Nursing, and recently achieved certification in machine learning and artificial intelligence from MIT. She holds a Bachelor's of Science in Nursing from the University of Rochester and a Master's of Science in Nursing from Boston College. Cheryl has been married over 30 years to her 3rd grade sweetheart Ted, and has three children Michael, Rebecca and Jennifer.

HEALING THE WOUNDS FROM OBESITY: A JOURNEY TOWARDS SELF

By Cheryl Field, MSN, RN, CRRN

I stepped on the scale and my ten-year-old self was ecstatic to see the indicator point directly at the large black number 80! I was "normal weight" for my height for the first time! The hard work of morning exercise, carbohydrate-free dieting, and dipping my urine to ensure I was in Ketosis had paid off. I did it! Growing up in the 1970s convinced me that aerobic exercise was the key to a slim, attractive, acceptable body shape. Combine excessive long-distance running with any number of fad diets, and all the success you wanted was yours for the taking! Or so I thought.

I was ten and overweight, thinking I could run off my excess weight. I began jogging two miles at dawn in the summer between fourth and fifth grade. I removed all carbohydrates from my diet and filled myself with salad and meat. I lost 17 pounds. My family said how great I looked. I entered fifth grade, met my first boyfriend, made new friends, and excelled at swimming and softball. I was sure the key to happiness was simply avoiding carbohydrates, exercising, and staying thin. Except as a ten-year-old there were birthday parties, school lunch programs, after school snacks, and celebrations where carbohydrates were routinely served, and sustaining ketosis was not possible. At this early age, I had a mixed-up relationship with hunger, food, overeating, and regret. I gained back all the weight that same year.

As an overweight kid in an overweight family, I thought all the problems in my family were due to obesity. My parents' divorce, my mother's prolonged single status, being cut from sports teams, and even our financial struggles. In my mind, the barrier to success was created by obesity. I was determined to change that generational obesity "curse" starting with my ten year old self. That year was not the only year I failed at sustaining normal weight. Numerous cycles of losing weight and gaining it back led to deep self-hatred, a loathing for parts of myself I did not understand.

For years I have lived with a constant battle in my head among different voices. The optimist and the pessimist, the scared and the critic. I was the master of negative self-talk any time I strayed one morsel from my diet plan. I would listen to an inner voice telling me I was sure to fail, and suddenly my choices and behaviors were consistent with that message. I questioned why I was not able to get this aspect of life under control. I ignored the deepest parts of myself, which felt alone and unlovable most of my young adult years. Only recently did I learn the trauma I experienced came from inside myself.

In the summer of 2021, I listened to a podcast called "The One Inside: An Internal Family Systems" hosted by Tammy Sollenberger, a licensed Internal Family Systems therapist. This day was the start of my healing journey. I became curious about those voices or different parts inside. I learned I could not run away from them. The IFS system helped me begin a journey to find peace within myself. I am still on that journey and committed to perfecting progress. The process required an inventory and acknowledgement of the validity and good intentions all my parts had. As I share my story with you, I hope you might begin your own healing journey.

When I tell my weight "story" struggle," I begin by saying, "I don't know how my mother managed to deliver me from her womb at 185 lbs." Truth is, 185 is the weight my body quickly settled at. I recall weighing 97 pounds in fourth grade and 80 pounds in fifth grade, my moment of "normal." I briefly recall weighing 150 for five minutes in middle school. Puberty carried with its rage of hormones a new set point, and my 13-year-old self learned to identify as a 185 pound "new born." From age 15 to today, I have gained and lost weight in 40-60 pound swings.

For most of my life, I tracked the major milestone events by how much I weighed. Not just my wedding day but parties, events, and other people's weddings were all tracked. The moment the invitation arrived, a part of me panicked. There was instant awareness of my current weight. A part of me set a goal weight, and the pressure was on. The date approached, and the weight had not been lost; deep personal disappointment set in. Many events were tainted by my inner critic scolding me for being unable to skip a few meals and look as good as everyone else. IFS taught me we each have an internal family system formed from such experiences. My parts were influenced by my chronic cycle of dieting, obesity, and society's messages about ideal body image.

Just recently, at age 55, I remembered a day from my freshman year of high school while taking an inventory of the parts inside me. That April, I was trying out for the school softball team. I desperately wanted to be on the team. On this day I would find out who the coaches chose by searching for my name posted on a list outside of the softball office door. Excited, optimistic, hopeful, and scared, I scanned the list for my name. It was not there. I had been cut. The reality of being rejected brought on feelings of sadness, followed by self-loathing. If only I had lost weight and looked like the other girls, I would have been accepted on the team. Full of anger, embarrassment, and shame, I left the softball office and headed outside; I would go for a run.

I don't really remember how long I was running before there were noticeably a lot of other student runners passing me. I said nothing, just ran at my normal slow pace. Before long, there was an adult pacing alongside me, and for a long while, we ran side by side in silence. Finally, he asked me how long I had been on the track team. My reply was short and angry.

"I'm not on the track team, I was just cut from the softball team." I snapped back at him. This angry, hurt, protective part was not interested in talking.

"Oh," he said. "I'm sorry, I thought you were a runner on the track team. You seem to have the heart of a runner."

"Really, you think I have the heart of a runner?" I said. "Well, I must have the body of something else," I responded in a self-loathing, self-deprecating tone. Some parts are just so persistent!

"I *do* think you have the heart of a runner. Why don't you join the track team? I'm the coach, and we could use someone with your passion on the team."

We ran along in silence again, and soon we were back at the school. I don't remember what I said next, I just know that some other part of me accepted the invitation, and I found myself on the team.

Track and Field was a team sport where an overweight teenage girl like me found some self-confidence. Weight was perceived as an asset in my events; shot put and discus. At the time, I attributed my frequent success to being overweight. I felt I was accepted and valued by the team members. At the end of the season banquet, I was stunned to be the recipient of the MVP award amongst the field eventers during my freshman year. I went on to receive this award for the next three years.

I sought out colleges where I could join the track and field team. When I arrived in the fall of 1985 to campus, I remember being shocked to meet *thin* teammates who were wildly successful in shotput and discus. I thought the secret to my success was the amount of weight I had behind me while throwing an object. Suddenly I was back on that softball field, embarrassed, self-loathing, and wondering why I couldn't manage my weight. "Why can't you be like these other athletes?" a part asked. I entered college weighing 188 pounds. I would leave for

Christmas break over 200 pounds. Upon returning in February, my coach took me aside to talk about a strength and conditioning program to help me reduce my excess body fat. Once again, I was facing an obstacle called obesity, and it was threatening the one space where I had found some acceptance and self-love.

Several cycles of weight loss and gain would consume my college years. I fell back on skills I had learned at ten years old and tried to lose weight by moving my body into ketoacidosis, and running extra miles before or after practice. I hid my shame and embarrassment from my friends, teammates, and family. Some days I was successful, other days I would order takeout and overeat. I was not getting the help I needed.

It's hard to be vulnerable and share how many painful parts I hide. I know now that we all have parts that need to be unburdened and need healing. The conversations in my head are repetitive. Different parts wrestled with low esteem and deep disappointment over my chronic struggle with obesity, often screaming at each other inside my head, all at once. For 40+ years I have been ashamed of my size, and I let the shame of obesity hold me back from doing things I wanted. "If only I was lighter," I would hear in my head as I made an excuse to avoid events.

Although I loved to go running – I hated the idea of people watching me run. I always wanted to sign up for 5k fundraisers or other charity events. I would sign up my children. We would go to the school for the event, and I would start running with them, but I would always hang back before we returned to the track where the finish line would be. I found an excuse never to cross the finish line. Obesity brought paralyzing negative body images and a profound fear of judgment I struggled to overcome.

I had been on my healing journey about three months when my daughter Rebecca decided she wanted to run the Disney Marathon.

She encouraged me to register for the ½ Marathon, which would take place the day before. Just the invitation sent my parts into battle in my head. I wanted to go for it, and a louder voice laughed me into shame. I put off registering for the event just long enough that it would be sold out. I truly regretted the decision.

I watched her run that Marathon in December of 2021, and she was amazing! I was her training partner and biggest fan. Even after six months of being on my own personal journey toward healing by learning about my Internal Family System, I felt the shame and disappointment build into a thundercloud in my head. Once again, I was letting that part of me that saw obesity as an obstacle dominate my choices. I was disappointed in myself. I made a lifetime of excuses, followed by self-loathing, overeating, and figuratively running away from the joy of living my life. I returned from Disney determined to work with my parts, to get closer to making choices from my centered self, versus allowing a blended part to choose for me.

Since listening to Tammy Sullenberger's IFS podcast, I sought out more IFS materials. I read the founder, Richard Schwartz's, *No Bad Parts* and Tammy Sullenberger's *The One Inside*. Being curious was the opening I needed. I began to see the self, which is separate from the parts; the self we can see and hear if we unblend from our parts. The exercises in the books were what started my healing. I would learn I needed to notice and listen to all my parts.

In April 2022, Rebecca asked me again to run a half marathon with her. I surprised my own self-critic part and said yes. I didn't tell many people about the race. The fear of ridicule and judgment came from parts within me. I established a training plan and decided to blend the ongoing practice assignments from *The One Inside* into my training time. I used my runs to get curious about my parts. I would begin a run and ask curiously, "Okay parts, who is here?" Most often, my scared part was first in line to say hello. This old familiar part was certain a ½ marathon was a bad idea. "What if you can't make it? Then what will the other parts say?" My scared part did not want my mean, judgmental, "You are going to fail," part to talk. Whatever part presented itself, I would invite it to join me up in the front of my mind. I would get curious and listen while we ran along.

It continued like this for me over the next few months of training as the long runs got longer. Being curious, I would invite my parts to 'come up front.' Sometimes I would find myself crying, listening, and comforting the parts I kept hidden away. There is a young girl who hides from the others I still don't really know much about. I have a very hungry part that wants to eat any time there are feelings of conflict, anxiety, or uncertainty. The more two parts disagree, the more aggressive the hungry part gets. My creative dancing part really liked the music in my headphones and wanted to be up front a lot. This part is happy and loves to dance. I ran my fastest mile split times when visiting with my creative part. I learned I had a strong part. This part could dig in deep and allow my legs to take another step after step. This part did not always like the long runs but would show up for moments when needed, like long hills and finishing sprints. My inner voice would hear my oldest daughter's words saying, "Come on legs," which was an invitation for my strong part to ride up front. Working on noticing the parts, thanking them for whatever job they have done to protect me, and just spending time together was an awakening. I never knew at the start of a run exactly which part of me would be there that day. The invitation was open, and they came as they desired.

About a month before the event, I learned the course had a time limit. Three hours and 15 minutes from start to finish for all runners. Anyone not at mile six by 90 minutes would be turned back around. Feelings of fear and embarrassment came rushing in. Would I be a person turned away from completing the race? My scared part was pounding in my chest. I almost backed out. Instead, three weeks before, with my youngest daughter Jennifer's company, I ran the first ten miles of the course to ensure that I could get to that sixth-mile mark in the allotted time. I knew that if I could get past this point, I would be allowed to finish the course. I also knew there might not be an actual finish line still set up when I did reach the finish. At that moment, my self was able to decide as long as I completed the half marathon, it didn't matter if there was an official finish line or not.

On the day of the race, I felt ready. I was finally taking a risk and pinning a number on my shirt, determined to run, jog, or walk every step of my own race. I was aware of some fear and anxiety debating with some confidence, creativity, and strength. I felt okay knowing all those parts of me would be with me on the course! In addition to my parts, several thousand people and my three children ran with me that day. My husband, sisters, and friends cheered for us along the way. It was the first time I overcame the obstacle of obesity and just ran for the joy of running for all to see. I completed the ½ Marathon in three hours and one minute, and over a proper finish line!

The journey I'm on will last a lifetime. I will continue to work on understanding, loving, and healing the parts inside using IFS. I have learned that for me to overcome the obstacles of obesity, I need to first do the work inside. Running gave me time and space to get curious and listen. I know I would never have finished the ½ marathon without the collective effort of all my parts. I hope that those reading this might find hope and healing through IFS. You are on your own journey. I know you can, and I know you will!

Dianne H Timmering

Elyon, LLC
American Author, National HealthCare Executive,
Global Entrepreneur

https://www.LinkedIn.com/in/dianne-timmering-1b35781a
https://www.facebook.com/Dhtimmering
https://www.instagram.com/Dharrison40/
www.Diannetimmering.com

Dianne H. Timmering, MFA, MBA, CNA, American Writer and Journalist, Healthcare Executive, Designer, Strategic Business Advisor, Start-up Entrepreneur, with sustainable ventures launched from ideation to implementation; a transformative leader, M&A contributor, national and local policy changer, spirituality "innovator," author, columnist, board member and builder of health and Virtual Care entities. A disruptive transformer, with decades of enterprise-wide experience, she Co-founded many entities including the Spirituality/Compassion Fund Pillar meeting the needs of thousands & served as SR VP of Healthcare Policy & Legislative Affairs for Signature HealthCARE, one of largest skilled post acute providers in U.S. with revenues of $1B+, with operations in 11 states. Bold and enduring, she is an effective leader with direct impact, creating businesses and taking on projects that require strategic design, fearless resilience, achieved performance benchmarks and tactical maneuvering resulting in revenue generation, including corporate growth and expansion. Ran the 2016 NYC Marathon and in 2014, hiked in 4-days the Inca Trail to Machu Picchu, and in 2009, the Milford Trek in New Zealand; also co-publisher of paper in 2011 on Spirituality and Its Value-Added Impact on Care Delivery & Revenue in healthcare.

IDENTITY

By Dianne H Timmering

I used to be important. I thought I really was.

My corporate identity was pasted on me like an invisible glue, and when I left my senior healthcare executive position in 2018, I was completely unaware of its all-consuming suction, the remains of my human identity stuck in the corporate vortex. When I tried to take it with me, it just wouldn't budge. It was there to stay, and waved me goodbye as I walked out the door.

The best way to describe it is like losing your human superpower.

I was leaving a generous company of learning, executive mobility, and spiritual freedom, but I had finished my executive and administering roles within the operating framework it had so graciously offered me. And I knew things. Healthcare things, like how private and public sectors and government policy all intersected to control day-to-day operations subjected to the limited mercies of regulatory and compliance oversight and often arbitrary reimbursement methodologies.

It was time to leave and take *thy* knowledge forth. I was going to save the world.

I mean, who in their right mind leaves an amazing billion-dollar healthcare enterprise I had helped build with many other incredible leaders? I mean, who leaves a revolutionary workplace into the sands of nowhere just because you know a few things?

But I was heady. A disrupter, I was ready to expand my healthcare impact across its many sectors—go enterprise-wide, from hospital to homecare, solving for challenges in the "health deserts" across our country, equalizing population health determinants, optimizing care delivery through virtual integrations, building entrepreneurial start-ups, and even working with state and federal governments to identify strategic metrics that could drive new codes of reimbursement.

Fearless, brave, a crusader for the vulnerable, a builder of new systems, a creator of intersections, I turned to the latest innovations which could sequence a reliable role into the deep epicenters of healthcare delivery--synthesizing data with technology, offering mental and virtual care in any setting, giving telehealth and virtual patient monitoring tools its early tactile role in the systemic healthcare process. And this was pre-Covid!

I was following a new North Star of purpose because I had lost it somewhere inside the crevices and corners of corporate walls. It just wasn't there anymore. I couldn't even find it under my desk or in an office drawer. It was almost like once you finish your purpose there, your role dissipates, and that associated identity starts to dissolve along with it, even as hard as you try to hold onto it.

The loss wrapped me up in an unexpected glumness like a kind of death, a naked rawness of a forced rebirth that I really didn't want anything to do with. I thought it would be an easy transition knowing I could do more for the healthcare industry. I thought a new call-to-purpose would replace one identity for another without a lot of conscious digging needed. But as I often was during this time, I was wrong.

Something inside of me was living in the deepest of secrets, this desire to effectuate a better well-being for the aging, prevent harsh sickness, and the often unnecessary consequences of it. But how to box-up all this fine new ambition into a sequential direction? I had to do the proverbial 'find the how-to' of this new purpose. Having a vision to build new worlds was one thing, but the map to get there was another.

Saying one needs to find purpose is an overused cliché—a small word for an often impossible endeavor. Purpose is a word we throw around, paddle it like a pickleball, smacking it back and forth into something that should mean something and yield a particular direction. But even saying all that, I desperately tried to find mine again. My job had ended, and I had punched that button on a new transformation trajectory. Just exactly what that was, and how to get there, I didn't know.

I knew I was on a good path because there was a tremendously large market for empire building. It wasn't just the technological bounty that was beginning to flood business markets, but the societal driver of a storming, norming, new, and older consumer base—the baby boomers were coming! 11,000 people were turning 65 a day. Tech savvy, these diverse humans demanded creative care with an early economic valuation based at $8 trillion big ones! "Aging" would become one of the largest global markets the world had ever seen. I could help make aging cool too!

Real live human healthcare data was also a big opportunity. So much of it was coming out, and as disparate as it was, there was the opportunity to do so much with it, integrate it into algorithms, and begin the path toward predictive medicine, identifiable patterns to monitor, and even prevent bad health episodes. Early monitoring meant getting better faster!

But big ideas need lots of direction. And not a lot of that was happening. I would get to the edge of each day, certain my next world mission had already been preserved in the timeline that each individual is born with, frozen until its time to thaw and break wide open. But there was no de-icing. I was an open promise with nowhere to go. I had moments of bravery, and many days of cowardice. But once you leave, there is no going back.

Like any entrepreneur, I am used to the word 'no,' or 'that can't be done,' or 'not now,' and pushing through it. But I had put my life and career on the frontline. I had listened to that small secret voice that we all carry, that divine credence within that tells you you're going the right way or the wrong one. I knew I had heard the voice to leave my corporate community, but now I was floating alone. And I was afraid. Even rage played a role for a time with the poetry of small violins playing self-pity on its tight belly of strings.

Now to be fair, as God does, he still showed up. I was able to secure a couple of impactful corporate national clients whose goals were similar to mine: to effectuate change, whether it was some kind of needed local policy overhaul, marketing local healthcare services, building wellness pilots, or incentivized innovative startup development to drive business economics within a wide city imprint. I was forever grateful to be a part of these missions, if only temporary. They were great morsels but small in the scope of what I intended to do and create for the world—real bedside healthcare 24/7—prevention, detection, healing, and reaching maximized revenue for the value-based care we would develop. I wanted to create, design, invent, and re-evolve national healthcare.

It all seemed like a really good plan.

But what wasn't I seeing? Why had I been pulled away into the ether of so much promise but had careened into little movement except for forced self-reflection, the kind that tunnels through to real soul development? Really uncomfortable stuff. It seemed easier to live in a half identity without having to knock on my head asking who was really in there.

We live in a life of pace and speed, not of self-reflection, which is why I think the pandemic was such a hard stop for us all, a reckoning with our mental states, stabbing at the mental conflict of expectation that binds us up in the cellophane of 'must-do' this and 'must-do' that.

Sometimes living and working in operable darkness is much easier than shifting our heads above the clouds and asking the real questions. What's next? What are my gifts? What do I need to actually be doing? How do I truly *realize every ounce of my being* (something I heard Sally Field say once)? How do I cut away what doesn't need to be there? Am I going the right way?

A newly seeded sadness settled, seeming to ebb and flow with the sun and its choice of appearance. Cloudy days were the hardest, especially when the phone calls didn't call back.

I had risked everything. I had listened to that steeled inner voice, but now even that voice had grown silent. I was there to rebuild "health deserts," but now I was in my own desert of hostility—sterile, dusty, never-ending, and with no way to build a house or find a well of water.

I had no office to go back to, and no remote working world existed at that point. My receptors were down, an empty soul staring me in the face. My identity was a victim of theft, and I didn't know how to get it back. This bred extreme grief. The brutal tones of unworthiness erupted inside any internal peace that I tried to find. And the temporary peace I could find inside the swishing of the drive-thru car-wash just wasn't doing it for me anymore.

One day I found myself on a distant road to an ancient Abbey in the rural valleys of Kentucky—a light transmission out of the gloom. I was glad to find that abbey road. I was glad to be on the way to somewhere, searching for the reasons behind lost wisdom, a broken heart, and scrambled purpose.

I drove along the byways of time through the landscape of lost corn and expended wheat. The sun bloomed through the shadows of trees, beckoning me on like it had opened up the day just for me. I was glad to be on the way and to be seen by the sun. The dance of winding roads and gentle hills of up and down stitched me up in that momentary peace, the kind that didn't yell at you to do better, do more, or try harder. And it was a way to go.

The road continued, a pilgrimage of dance, like life should be a dance and somewhere along the way I had forgotten to get on the floor and boogie. The air was cold, but inside the car was warm, even hot enough to have me push my visor down both from the bounding sun and the consuming anticipation of what was secretly tucked inside those hills of Nelson County, Kentucky. Somewhere there was an ancient past laced in the dales of centuries, a vortex of an alien world where I hoped solace could be found and that Lost Voice could be heard again.

The climb there seemed to be a long tunneling doorway leading to God's middle, a place where he could summon the angels, view plights on the plains of the planet, and send out his warriors with orders of protection, hope, and light.

The river was high from too much rain as I crossed a narrow bridge glossed with ice from the night before. A herd of tall trees crowded both sides of the riverbed, their toe trunks wet from the swelling rains. Those on the left bank seemed to have attempted an escape but had gotten stuck in the earth before they could make a clean getaway to the other side.

They struck laughter in me in the golden light of the morning, like they were hunched over in their getaway slump of disappointment. I had a kinship with them because I was stuck too, and if they could flee, where would they go? Maybe I could hitch a ride in their limbs, nest alongside the colorful birds, and sleep inside a halo of branches.

How do I find an identity I accidentally lost? How do I find my way again? So much to do, nowhere to do it.

The wandering road rolled out before me. I knew it was there by the rat-a-tat-tat under the tires, but it didn't give me too far to see in its distance. Trust the road. A left turn here, a right turn, a generous curve there, a tobacco barn, and of course a bourbon factory, close enough to find its way into the fudge that monks could make. Bourbon delights could find themselves in any recipe, especially in the commonwealth of Kentucky. Hopefully, if there was a gift shop, I could find some to buy.

I pulled into the demure driveway of the Abbey, my car a capsuled transport like a spaceship that had found heaven for the day and was coming in for an easy landing. It was as if this enclave on the hill was some kind of portal to a realm, a kind of Jacob's ladder, where good angels could come and go and find their assignments on this earth—of comfort or battle. They would find their "person" and be only for that one, like God was sending a rescue as it says in Psalms 91 – *"shout out and He will come, He will send help; He will rescue in a time of trouble."*

Why don't more people ask for help? Why hadn't I?

The structures were not more sophisticated than its decades-old build—angular and vanilla, utilitarian and orderly like the days of each minute and meal for every monk who lived there. The beauty of the place didn't come just from the architecture of its pleasant gardens, streaming land, simple shapes, and muted colors, but from sparked energy that God was somehow present in the perimeter that surrounded the dwellings of the visitor center, lodging, chapel, and sanctuary.

I was drawn to the small auditorium for a memoir reading by a monk, so full of aura. I was the only listener to sit in the front row because I wanted whatever it was he had. I wanted the peace that blended into his tunic and the fabric of his garb, and in his words from a life lived—meditating daily outside—including during the deepest scars of winter. I wanted to soak in his straddle of this world and the next, like he was wading in the ocean's warm waters where God seems to hold many of His earthly secrets. I listened on the edge of the pew, a wooden seat that sculpted my rear into the polygon of straight lines forcing back up and bottom flat—deliberate without luxury but oh so rich.

Monk Paul Quenon began to read.

> *I take Mother Nature as my spiritual teacher, tough and gentle. I stay at her feet through each year's long, twelve-month lesson... If the temperature is four above zero, I'm out there... sometimes this calls for endurance but no more than a farmer tending the cows.* <u>In Praise of the Useless Life</u>

This lovely monk lived in a deliberate kind of consciousness, a kind of awareness that is so hard to find, maybe because we are so busy avoiding it as we live out our daily routines. Even in the severest days, Monk Quenon had found a way to his solace and could hear the mysteries of daily living and guided pursuits.

Afterward, swollen gloves captured loose tears as I made my way to the 19th century chapel, which looked like a domed adobe long and indestructible, old and sacred. Walking in—the Throne beckoned forth.

> *It is with every ordinary person in the world intoxicated and distracted by self-grasping, completely in bondage to a limited and mortal self-identity, and so remaining under the power of death. Yet, if one can let go... one will remember what has been forgotten and so set oneself free.* <u>Gnostic Gospel of St. Thomas, Meditations of Mystical Teachings</u>, Tau Malachi

And there It was, in the sturdiness of the throne, the softness of the monk's tender words, and the tears of surrender. I could be free of the neglect of the present; I was also free to detach from the identity of my past. And in that moment of nothing, direction began to filter in again. The Light Transmission began to fire into the mission and organized purpose of a reformed soul.

Behind any business model is the precious human at the end of it. Don't forget My people. Healthcare is not just based on volumes but My person. Each one.

I had reset. I was awake, like this complexly simple monk, knowing I didn't need to cling to an old identity of old ambition. The monk's joy hadn't come from the daily life he led but from living in deep attentiveness to it.

Inside the quiet, I too, could hear again.

I could leave the struggling self behind because there was a new one to wear even though it wasn't fully unveiled yet. I required a new fitting, an evolving identity like a newly knitted coat made of different patterns, delicate stitching, and unique fabrics. Directions re-surfaced, strategic co-partners revealed, and obtainable business models written. And I was writing again.

After his memoir reading, I went up and hugged the monk, telling him I didn't need to meditate in four-degree mornings. I would leave that kind of open coolness to him!

By Dianne H. Timmering, MBA, MFA, CNA

Annette Kruschek

https://www.facebook.com/akruschek
https://momsapplecart.weebly.com/
https://youtube.com/@SolelyInspired

Annette Kruschek's life is a tapestry woven with equal parts of family, marriage, faith and grief. As a devoted wife and mother to eight children, including three with congenital heart defects, Annette has experienced the joys and complete despair with raising a large family.

Tragically, one of Annette's children lost her life at a young age of four due to complications from her condition. Annette continues to find solace in her faith. Through her writing and blogging Annette shares her journey of navigating grief while finding hope in the aftermath of tragedy. Her message of resilience and determination has inspired readers all over the world.

Annette remains committed to her family and personal pursuits. She has completed eight marathons, tends to her hobby farm, and upcycles antiques, all while raising her children.

Annette is a beacon of hope for others who may be struggling to find their way forward.

MY TINY TEACHER

By Annette Kruschek

In a rural and poor city, in the backroom of an overpacked and understaffed orphanage, God handpicked an "outcast," an "unlikely," and an "underdog" of a child… he chose my daughter, Evelyn Li. This is a story about life, death, and the pursuit of meaning and hope while coming to terms with living with grief and loss on a daily basis.

From the moment Evelyn entered our lives, she demanded time: our time, the doctor's time, God's time. Time, what a gift that created memories, laughter, healing, and hope for a future. Time, a sudden thief that barged in in the middle of the night, stole our light, and left us breathless. The hands of the clock stood still just as Evelyn's body stood still on February 25, 2021, leaving my husband and her seven siblings to beg for more time with her. It still doesn't seem real that I will live the rest of my life without my youngest child. If I could possess any superpower, it would be to hoard time with Evelyn and never let it go.

Evelyn passed away at the young and innocent age of four years old. My husband and I adopted Evelyn when she was 18 months old. Evelyn was born with a rare and complicated heart condition. From the moment I met Evelyn, I felt deep within my heart that she was on her own personal mission, a mission to truly love. I quickly realized that I became the student in Evelyn's life and was gifted the front-row seat in her classroom.

Over the course of sitting in Evelyn's classroom, her family, friends, and perfect strangers from around the world were given the rare opportunity to watch a malnourished 13-pound child undergo the biggest and most incredible transformation. Evelyn underwent multiple risky heart surgeries that were unique and tailored to her very specific physiology. With each successful surgery came an awareness of this child's assignment of drawing people into her spirit. If you were fortunate enough to be a student in her classroom, you were changed for the better. Someone said it well when describing their relationship with her: "I never personally met Evelyn, but her spirit and light hooked me in and I couldn't get enough." If you were in Evelyn's presence it was like sitting in the front row of the most beautiful love story. With each love story, you must sacrifice and humble yourself to that person you love so dearly. Evelyn made you put your toes to the ledge, climb mountains, be a risk taker, and most of all, appreciate time. While Evelyn's time here on earth was cut tragically short, she accepted one of the most difficult invitations: to be used by God and say yes to his will for her life.

My husband said something so powerful only days after she passed away. He said, "Maybe it was as if she knew her time was limited, and she didn't want any of us wasting ours." From the moment she came home from China, Evelyn got all of us. I let her dance on the kitchen counter, and I sang out loud without any embarrassment because it was for Evelyn. She allowed our entire family to sing and dance our way into her life. My husband sang Edelweiss to Evie before bed, without fail. The day she passed, Dan and I held her close while Dan sang it for the final time. She made us present in every detail of her life. Even the little things, Band-aids, makeup, a specific song list, her beloved baby pillow, and her sweet little voice when she demanded that her entire family crowd around and give a "family hug." Thankfully our entire family realized what a gift Evelyn was, so we handled her with care. It was because of this that I think we all would agree that we have zero regrets about our time with her. In the depths of my soul and the pit of my heart, I now realize that God never promised me Evelyn's healing here on earth. I've said time and time again that God is not a vending machine where you insert a prayer and choose the best outcome. Over the past ten years, I have suffered many losses: my father, my mother, and my brother. Deep down inside, I think I was worried that God was preparing me for one of the biggest losses... the death of my child.

I can see now, while looking back to my childhood, God was also preparing me, stretching me, and growing my faith. I have two interesting confessions to make. Confession number one, I was terrified of my parents dying. I equate my anxiety of death to that of having older parents. I was born when my parents were 45 (it's ironic because I was 44 when Evelyn was born in China). The seed of fear had been planted at a young age, and I never knew how to conquer it, so death was not my friend. Confession number two, as a child, I was always picked last. In my generation, it was common to "pick teams" during Phy Ed class or recess. I vividly remember how my peers would eagerly await their names being called, validating that they were "chosen" to be on their beloved team. The pool of kids would eventually dwindle to the "not-quites" and then the remaining few (me included) would become a bargaining tool where the captains would go back and forth with who would get the "leftovers." Torture is the best way to describe those moments. I was the girl picked last, the leftover, the "not quite." God scripted my story with Evelyn even as I was a young child. Never did I believe that I would not only come face to face with a child who was seen as an outcast but also as an underdog in the largest medical sense of the word.

I am not brave, friends. I am one of the "not-quites", the girl who swims against the current, the one who many see as a "bible thumper." I am one of God's chosen, and that is a team that I am proud to be on. Whether you are picked first or last, God will always find a spot for you on his team. YOU have a purpose. YOU have meaning. YOU are going to be used spectacularly if you allow him to use you. I can now reflect on the past ten years at all the losses that I have endured and know that God never wasted any of my pain, fear, and hurt. I can confidently say that the harder my walk with God, the more authentic it has become. I've realized that he knows me and used my fear of death to show me I can carry it with his help. He continues to transform me from the inside out. Let me be very clear, though, the pain I feel every day without having a little hand to hold, a tiny voice calling me Mommy, is the most difficult pain I have ever endured, and I would give anything to change God's will for our family.

Living with grief while being a mother to seven kids and a husband of 25 years has been extremely difficult. The day Evelyn passed, the light in our family went out. I will not sugarcoat any of this. Never in a million years did I imagine my husband and I holding our daughter in an emergency room, making three phone calls to our kids, and letting them know that their sister had unexpectedly passed away. We had three horrible phone calls to make, one to Evelyn's oldest sister in college, the other to her oldest brother while he had his arms wrapped around three other siblings in our kitchen, and finally the last one to my husband's parents since two of our kids were having a sleepover at their home. My husband had to repeat the terrible news three separate times. Helpless, traumatic, and tragic. That is how the journey has felt while trying to keep our family afloat. There were many days when all I felt like I was doing was holding spinning plates. In my mind, I was running to each plate to keep it moving because the fear of one falling on the ground and crashing was too much to bear. I have learned through much therapy that I cannot take anyone's pain away. No matter how much quality time I spend with them or laughter I share with them, the pain is their own, and it isn't until they have journeyed through the feelings that they will begin to confront their grief head-on.

I have learned something universal and similar to my kids and their grief; they are all watching my husband and I. It's like living in a small fishbowl some days because they are looking to us to see how we are handling the loss of Evelyn. My kids are so wise, and no matter how often I tried to hide my emotions, they would become the caretaker to one another to make things "easier." It has taken a lot of open communication and honesty to permit everyone to tell the truth about what we need and when we need it. You cannot put grief off for another time. Placing it on the back burner is like watching a pot of boiling water boil over and make a mess of everything in its sights. I have learned to grieve in front of my kids because I am teaching them how to grieve on their own. Not one of my kids has grieved the same. Therapy has helped me love each child where they are in their journey. In the last two years, the only thing that Evelyn's death has positively taught me was to be very intentional with each child. Quality time, intentional moments, raw conversations, and brutal honesty has made my bond with each one stronger and much more authentic. Because of my kids, I found myself getting out of bed each morning. Because of them, I realized I needed to continue living. Because of them and their dependency on my husband and I, I wasn't about to let Evelyn's death dictate how I lived the rest of my life. Honoring Evelyn while being the best Mother I can is a God-given gift that I will never take for granted.

Grief is a very ugly giant. It trampled over my family and stomped on a very strong marriage. My husband and I have been married for 25 years. We met at the young age of 18, and I can honestly say he has been my best friend since the day I laid eyes on him and his crazy haircut. One would think that we have endured seasons of difficulties with our marriage and relationship, but that was seldom the issue. We agreed on many things. We were a great team in situations that tested not only our stamina to raise such a large family but also our commitment to caring for my ailing parents. I guess you could say the more life threw at us, the more we would find a way to run with it and not look back. Then February 25, 2021 hit, and as the hands of time stopped, the image of my marriage came to a shocking halt. Sadness eventually turns to anger if not fully repaired. Anger in itself is really fear. Fear sets in rather quickly after a loved one passes. For me, the fear was wondering if I could physically handle the heartache. Fear of learning how to live differently and, in terms of my marriage, fear of losing my husband. There were days that I didn't know how we would find our way back to one another again. Our past experiences of jumping in headfirst and tackling problems together didn't even come close to helping us with the death of Evelyn.

During those months of despair and often silence, I learned something.

I didn't have a lightbulb moment, quick fix, or magic pill. I literally lifted my hands and found myself praying throughout the day. My prayers were neither rote nor saved for bedtime or those designated for church. I remember walking out in the woods one day after feeling misunderstood and almost laughing, saying to God, "Why? I'm here and I'm asking for help, but you continue to push me... why?" By the time I finished my walk, I felt as if my one-way conversation with God suddenly had a faint voice talking back to me. It was a glimmer of clarity that I can't claim I came up with, but rather a seed God placed in my hand. Since that day months ago, I named that my "seed of sorrow." I felt as if the voice I heard was God whispering the word "expectant." I took that word as my glimmer of hope and tucked it within my heart.

"Expectant"... I was expecting God to answer my prayers. I was expecting my marriage to rebuild itself onto a new foundation after the monster of grief came rushing in. My prayers and conversations with God have never ceased. I pray with anticipation and expectation that he will move mountains just as he had done in the past. Evelyn's passing is not an indication that my prayers weren't answered. I saw firsthand how God moved mountains for her and through her. I saw

God bring people to their faith, and I felt God in every aspect of her life. That is hard to explain to those who struggle with their faith, but as a Mother to Evelyn and a child of God, it is not for me to judge God's ways. It is only important that I remain steadfast with who God is and will be forever. In terms of my marriage, God knew that Dan and I would struggle, but through the fires of grief we are finding our way back to each other. The fires of grief have only burned off what was not intended for our marriage and my family. I have learned that being completely vulnerable with my husband and children is beautiful.

I gave my marriage and my children to God for him to manage and repair. I need to be more silent to see and hear his plans for us all. I take zero credit. I will always give credit to prayer and patience when God is in control. Evelyn's death didn't define our marriage, nor the legacy of our family. Her life here on earth gave us the strength to make sure we shine her light brightly so that it draws people to her spirit in heaven.

I thank God every day for allowing me another day to live side by side with my best friend and beautiful children. That small seed God placed in my hand during that walk in the woods has been gently planted. The seed of sorrow is emerging into a bud of steadfast love.

Evelyn will continue to live inside all of us. Evelyn coined a very special phrase," I SO BRAVE." I believe she passed the torch of her bravery to our entire family. We all honor her by carrying that torch until we see her and her messy pigtails again. I hope my words of grief and sorrow have fallen in a safe place within your mind and heart. You are not alone, and the pain that you may be experiencing does have a purpose. The purpose of my pain is one that I am still uncovering. My prayer for you is this, find purpose in the pain and strength in the trenches of grief that you may be walking. You are never alone.

Adrienne Kennie

CEO & Founder of 28th State Business Solutions

https://www.linkedin.com/in/adrienne-kennie-80ab3327
https://www.facebook.com/adrienne.kennie
https://instagram.com/msnikki_81?igshid=ZDdkNTZiNTM=

Adrienne Kennie was born and raised in Austin, Texas where she currently resides. She received a Bachelors of Science degree in Health Administration from Texas State University and a Masters degree in Business Administration from Concordia University. She also completed the Women's Entrepreneurship program with the Bank of America Institute at Cornell University. She is currently a Management Consultant for a large consulting firm. During her free time she enjoys spending time with family and friends, making arts and crafts, traveling, writing and most of all her role as mom to her one year old daughter. Adrienne is the CEO and Founder of 28th State Business Solutions, LLC and is currently working on other projects to promote her passion and goals to help others. Adrienne is also a co-author of Shattering the Stigma of Single Motherhood.

FINDING PEACE WITHIN

By Adrienne Kennie

This Can't Be Real

There are some things in life that we will never be prepared for. On January 9, 2018, I finished my workday and decided to get a manicure and pedicure. I arrived at the nail shop, and as I was sitting in the chair, I felt uneasy. My stomach was in knots, and I couldn't sit still because I felt something was wrong, but I couldn't pinpoint exactly what "wrong" was. After having this feeling for 30 minutes, thoughts of my brother instantly hit me, and I could feel that something was wrong with him. It was so strange because I could feel my brother's presence with me at that very moment. I frantically picked up my phone and began calling him repeatedly but couldn't reach him because the phone instantly went to voicemail.

I then received a call from his friend, who mentioned that my brother was supposed to pick him up from work but never made it. I left the nail shop and met my brother's friend at his job. My brother still hadn't arrived. His friend received a phone call that an accident was broadcast on the news, and my brother could have potentially been involved. We rode to the hospital, and as we walked through the entrance doors, a police officer stopped us and informed us that my brother didn't survive the accident and passed away at the scene. There were two other passengers. One died the next day, and the other was comatose for six months and unfortunately passed away. I was devastated and in complete shock, but I felt as if I had to make sure arrangements were taken care of, so I pushed forward and went to the funeral home to ensure that my brother was taken care of. My brother and I were close. He was my best friend. I always appreciated that I could ask him for advice, and he would always be honest with me and never sided with me just because I was his sister. If I were wrong, he would tell me I was wrong. Siblings are the very first friends you have in life, and I never thought I would have to figure out how to live without any of them, yet here I was, having to figure out how I was supposed to continue without my younger brother.

I continued to push forward, wrote my brother's obituary, compiled photos, made countless calls to make sure things were in order for the service, and my on-and-off boyfriend helped me pick my brother's suit. I was always the one who was responsible for making sure everyone in the family was okay, and I was determined to make sure my brother was okay as he was laid to rest. About a week after my brother's funeral, I was scheduled to take a trip to visit my best friend in Arizona. I woke up the morning of my flight feeling horrible. I had a sore throat, headache, extreme fatigue, and it took everything to get out of bed. I knew I could not board the plane, but needed to see a doctor. Luckily my primary doctor had same-day availability, and I could get an appointment. When my doctor walked into the examination room and asked me how I was doing, the meltdown happened. I started crying uncontrollably in the office. The doctor sat with me as I cried and tried to explain what happened. I had anxiety, depression, and the flu, which was the reason for the appointment. I guess the shock had worn off, and I was no longer in denial. My brother was really gone, and somehow, I had to accept it.

Just Keep Moving... Somehow

I continued pushing forward and carried on with life the best way I could. I disagreed with the guy that I was dating on and off again, and we were off again. This was the pattern throughout the years. When things were good, they were good; when they weren't, we simply didn't communicate. I knew that this wasn't healthy, but I kept pushing forward. I was working for a health insurance company, and I was happy with this job because I could get most of my work done in the morning, and I had downtime in the afternoon. I knew I wasn't challenged, but I was okay with not being stressed and being able to leave at 5 PM every day. For years I thought more and more about buying my first home and started saving money for the down payment. I limited my social life and activities, and I reached my goal down payment amount. Unfortunately, when I started the application process, I was denied because I had co-signed on a car for my brother, which caused an increase in my debt-to-income ratio, and I didn't have the income needed to make the purchase. I knew I needed to challenge myself to accomplish my goal.

As I approached the new year, I was hoping that things would improve, but somehow 2019 began with sadness for my family. My aunt passed away on New Year's Day, and subsequently, my friend passed away after collapsing suddenly the following month. I began to understand how precious life is and how it can be gone in an instant. One afternoon, I had finished my shift, and I received a call from a recruiter with a large consulting firm. I hadn't applied for the position and wasn't sure how the recruiter found me, but I agreed to meet with the hiring managers to discuss a consulting role. After two initial meetings, they flew me to Chicago, and I interviewed with the Senior Manager and Managing Director of the healthcare practice. I was offered a consulting position on the spot. I received a pay increase and was told that the job would require traveling weekly, Monday–Thursday. I was extremely excited about the opportunity and gratefully accepted it in April.

I started traveling every week for work and visiting various cities. At first, this was fun, and it was nice to travel and explore new cities, but as time passed, it began to get old quickly. The position paid more and challenged me more than any position I ever had, but I felt as if I was living out of a suitcase. I knew it was time to start looking for a home again because I needed this sacrifice to count. In May, my uncle began to get sick and was hospitalized. He was battling cancer, and things were not looking good. My grandmother was also in hospice, and our family was preparing for the end. When I was in town, I spent many days visiting my uncle in the hospital and my grandmother in hospice. In June, I received a call that my dad was severely ill and taken to the ER via ambulance. When I spoke with my dad's doctor, she expressed that my dad had a severe spinal infection that could have been deadly if he wasn't brought in. Somehow, I managed to continue working, traveling from Austin to Phoenix, and traveling from multiple hospitals and hospice facilities to check on my uncle, grandmother, and father while I was in town. During lunch break or after work, I consistently called to check on my dad and make decisions as needed because he was in a rehab facility for several months. While visiting with my uncle one night, we talked for a few hours, and my uncle told me that I should leave because it was getting late. I'm not sure why this day felt different, but I gathered my things, said goodbye to my uncle, and told him I would come back to visit him. I walked out the door, but as I took a few steps, I felt the need to turn around and walk back to the room. I opened the door and asked my uncle if he would be okay. He looked at me, said he would be fine, and told me to go home. Within a few hours, my uncle went into respiratory arrest and was placed in a medically induced coma. The doctors stated that this was the end, and the family decided to take him off of life support. My family gathered together, prayed, and said goodbye to my uncle. Two months later, my grandmother passed away a week before her 93rd birthday. This was such a rough time, and I struggled to find balance, but I had to keep going.

The Breaking Point

The guy I was dating returned in August of that year, and we started conversing again. In September, I was out driving and decided to look at model homes. I checked out a few and found a beautiful home that I LOVED! I decided to try the homebuying process again, and this time, I was approved. I signed a contract for a new build and waited patiently for my home to be ready. My dad was doing so much better and was able to return home. When I closed on my home, I was beyond excited. This was during Covid, and travel stopped completely with my job. Covid was an extremely scary time, but I found relief knowing I could work from home and not travel every week. I was completely burnt out from all of the traveling. I moved into my home and started settling into homeownership.

In March 2021, I found out that I was pregnant. The guy I dated on and off again was not in the best place, and things were difficult. We lived in two different cities, which made things challenging when it came to going to doctor's appointments together, or the little things like having someone get peanut butter and pickles in the middle of the night for cravings, but I pushed through. I went to a routine doctor's appointment at 34 weeks with extremely high blood pressure. My doctor sent me to labor and delivery immediately, and after hours of no progress, I had an emergency C-section that night. I saw my baby briefly before she was taken to the NICU. My blood pressure didn't stabilize for several days, and I couldn't see or hold my baby until three days later. When we were able to go home, I was so excited. Being a new mom was an adjustment, as I was healing from the C-section, breastfeeding, waking up throughout the night, etc. It was a struggle initially, but things started getting easier. Thankfully I had time off because I could not imagine trying to adjust to motherhood and working at the same time.

I returned to work after maternity leave, which was quite an adjustment. Being a single parent is definitely not for the weak. I was working all hours of the day and night just to make sure I was meeting the demands of the job and managing motherhood at the same time. I began to realize that I was extremely overwhelmed and didn't feel I was performing my best at work. This was new for me because I always excelled at work. Still, I felt as if a block was preventing me from fully focusing on work, and I felt as if I was being forced to choose between being the best that I could be at work and being the best mother I could be.

I began to feel extremely sad more days than I felt happy. One day I was working on a proposal for work that required the team to be all hands on deck. We had a meeting one evening from 6 PM-9 PM and then worked on a powerpoint until 2 AM. I then slept until 6 AM, made additional changes in preparation for the upcoming meeting at 8 AM, and somehow managed to get my daughter up, fed, and dressed for daycare. By the time I returned home, I was exhausted, crying and knew I was in the red zone. I knew I couldn't continue working like this, but I felt an overwhelming pressure to work as hard as I needed because I felt a large weight on my shoulders as a single parent.

Shattering the Stigmas and Finding Peace

I began to feel hopeless and felt as if I was drowning. I felt an overwhelming need to excel in corporate America as a black woman and felt that in order to excel, I needed to go above and beyond or work harder than my counterparts. I didn't feel safe raising my hand and saying I was struggling because I didn't want to be perceived as weak. In addition, I felt that I had failed in my love life. I always wanted to be married, but I was now a single mom. I was in an off-and-on relationship that brought no sense of security, and I didn't feel it was going anywhere. I was also experiencing loss after loss, and I didn't allow myself grace and time to process and fully grieve. All of these things were holding me back, and I didn't know how to move forward. I was starting to crumble, and it was showing in my everyday life. I started gaining weight and wasn't going out anymore. Finding anything to smile about was harder and harder, and I knew I needed to seek counseling.

I took some time off from work and focused on my mental health. I spent some time processing prior and current events in my life and sought to understand why I kept aligning myself with situations that weren't bringing me true happiness. I discovered that I was not living my purpose and was simply living a life based on the expectations of others. I was on a journey of healing and started to be honest with myself about what I wanted and how I would live on my terms. I even found that the weight slowly started to come off. I allowed myself time and grace to grieve the losses I encountered. I also learned the importance of setting healthy boundaries and sticking to my wants and needs without feeling the need to sacrifice them. I began to appreciate the beauty of life and didn't feel the need to sacrifice myself to fit in the box of corporate America or wear the strong woman cape while suffering. I found that true strength is making sure you are whole and getting the help you need to do so. One day I woke up feeling so much clarity and knew I was ready to start living again because I had finally found peace.

Dedication

I dedicate my story to my forever angels: Derrick Kennie, Lillie Mae Kennie, Dorothy Richards, Lessie Mitchell, Julian Mitchell, Wanda Mitchell, Ronnie Conner, and Cayce Stevenson.

Kat O'Sullivan

KAT O'SULLIVAN
Keynote Speaker | Author | Lifelong Changemaker

https://www.linkedin.com/in/make-magic-happen
https://www.facebook.com/KathleenOSullivanProfile
www.katosullivan.com

Kat O'Sullivan believes when shift happens, it's time to make magic happen. She is known for doing the seemingly impossible over and over again. Kat inspires people to move toward the future that's just waiting for them to say, "Hell, Yes!" to what they really want and create new possibilities.

Kat's journey as a lifelong changemaker began when she was only 16. She was selected for the once-in-a-lifetime opportunity to travel with Up With People, sharing a message of hope and goodwill through a powerful two-hour musical performance. Kat called Bob Hope, convinced him to sponsor her travels, and hit the road.

Most recently, Kat wanted to build a new life and enjoy every moment with her husband. They packed up their entire life and made a major move to a foreign country – in the middle of a pandemic. They are now embracing an exciting, rejuvenating new way of life.

ANSWERING THE CALL

By Kat O'Sullivan

God's ways are rarely our ways, and He often has an uncanny sense of humor. Never in my wildest imagination could I have anticipated how answering an unexpected call back in 1988 would turn into my 'calling' and my lifeline.

It's 9:00 pm. I hear an anxious voice, "Kat, this is Terri. I just found out my two-year-old Mikey has a malignant brain tumor. They're operating in the morning, and I'm scared. Can you come to the hospital?"

I'd like to say that my immediate thought is, "Of course," but I barely know Terri. Why is she calling ME? It's as if time stands still, and I'm sure it's only seconds, yet it feels like hours. An internal battle rages as fear begins to take hold. Everything within me screams, "NO!" At the same time, there is a still, small voice urging me to go.

The next thing I know, I'm making the 20-minute trek through the dark and somewhat ominous canyon between my home and the hospital—a metaphor for what I'm about to experience.

Imagine, I step off the elevator and enter the "twilight zone" . . . the pediatric oncology unit. Everything is totally foreign. I'm second-guessing my decision and getting ready to flee when Terri throws her arms around me. Sobbing, she says, "I don't know how to do this. I'm five months pregnant. My husband and I need to keep working, or we'll lose our health insurance." My emotions are all over the place, and this isn't even my child.

It feels like Terri's dilemma is becoming mine as well. As I drive home, I'm bargaining with God about my role in this unfolding drama. God, you know how much I hate hospitals and doctors. Why me? Why now?

You know the struggles I'm facing. This feels like more than I can handle. I'm pulling into our driveway, questioning whether I can be courageous enough to answer the 'call' when a surprising peace washes over me.

The next morning, I stepped off that same hospital elevator. Kids are walking around with IV poles as if it's normal. It's surreal. I find Mikey's room and hear myself saying. "Hey Terri, I'm working on the weekends. What if I sit with Mikey during the day while my kids are at school?" I think, did I just say that? Terri's response is one of overwhelming gratitude.

For the next six weeks, I feel like I'm living in an alternate universe. Young children are walking around the unit, IV pole in hand. It's as if they don't know that their 'normal' isn't normal at all! It's amazing how they find joy in the littlest thing when death is at their doorstep for many.

I can't help but notice a small gaggle of girls, five and six-year-olds, hanging out together. They hate being mistaken for boys. Their bald heads and unshapely figures betray them. Girly stuff to the rescue! I bring in make-up, headbands, and jewelry for them to play with . . . anything that will help them look and feel like the beautiful girls they are.

I am particularly intrigued by one girl who always seems to be on the periphery and has no visitors. I learned that Vanessa's parents abandoned her four months earlier—just before Christmas. Unthinkable! She had been diagnosed with a life-threatening and aggressive brain tumor like Mikey's. Vanessa had been going through surgery and gruesome high-dose chemo and radiation for over four months already, with no family support. Her courage inspires me to let go of my fear and allows courage to take hold.

I wonder, am I here for Mikey or Vanessa, or in some way for me?

While I didn't realize it at the time, Vanessa and I were living parallel lives of desperation and, over time, restoration. It changed everything for me, Vanessa, and everyone on our path.

I make time to connect with Vanessa.

Then comes the fateful night. Vanessa's recent chemo is taking a deadly toll. The nurses call her family, but they never show up. I decide to stay. I hold her hand through the night, determined that this precious child will not die alone. Miraculously she survives. Somehow, I know her life and mine will never be the same. We have an unbreakable bond.

A few days later, I asked the nurses if I could take her to the park or McDonald's to get her out of the hospital for a few hours. Their response? "That's impossible."

Three days later, Sandy, a social worker, approaches me and asks if I will take Vanessa. My immediate response is, "To the park?" knowing she really means take her home. The moment of truth: will I succumb to my fear or be courageous enough to trust this is meant to be? When I say, "Yes," Sandy shares it will probably only be for about three months, which is how long they expect her to live.

Everyone thinks I'm crazy.

You might be thinking the same thing.

A week later, I'm loading Vanessa into my van and maneuvering the twists and turns of the canyon, yet again wondering what the bleep I'm doing.

I'm facing a harsh reality. Everyone in my life thinks it's crazy, and they distance themselves from the potential loss. The only exception is a dear friend, Catt. "Listen, Kat, when Vanessa's time on earth is over, you'll have the privilege of ushering her back into the arms of God." That gives me a whole new perspective and the courage to face what lies ahead.

While saying "Yes!" to Vanessa seems crazy, it feels more and more like a "calling." Little do I know it will be my saving grace, literally. After bringing her home, I experience the best of times and the worst of times. I am stretched to my breaking point. I'm giving out of an empty, bone-dry cup.

Being at the hospital is a bizarre reprieve from troubles on the home front, where I'm feeling utterly invisible. I have spent my life trying to please everyone. In hindsight, I wonder if taking Vanessa is my way of proving I am somehow worthy of love and approval. My people-pleasing is a useless pursuit with devastating results in my marriage. I realize it is a perfect marriage . . . of dysfunction, that is.

I find myself in my therapist's office with a purse full of enough pills to end the pain permanently. Randy asks me a question that shakes me to my core, "Kat, do you see any parallels between Vanessa's life and your own? Abandoned, no support . . . dying?" He goes on, "While others may have abandoned you throughout your life, can you see that you are contemplating the ultimate abandonment . . . of yourself?" Ouch! He is right.

I have a choice: admit myself, or be admitted. I wonder if God knew that it would take all of this for me to finally get the support I will need for what is still to come.

I affectionately call my time in the hospital my forty days in the desert. It is a safe place, and I feel seen and heard for the first time. It renews my faith and my belief that I am worthy of being loved and that I can experience grace for abandoning myself for all those years. I can also extend grace to others who abandoned me, realizing they were doing the best they could. I leave with the clarity, commitment, and courage I need to end that perfect marriage of dysfunction. I realize that as a single mom, I have the opportunity to reparent myself by parenting Vanessa how I always wanted to be parented. Maybe it would even help me parent my son, Jeff.

Amazing what happens when I let go of the fear that's been holding me captive.

Fast forward, I'm finishing dinner in a restaurant that exudes romance. Imagine the most beautiful bouquet of flowers coming into the room. I know they couldn't be for me, but I wish they were. Then I feel everyone's eyes on me as the bouquet comes closer and closer. Then I see a baseball seated like a nest in the middle of a sea of red roses. Only Michael, the ultimate romantic, could dream up a moment like this.

My first encounter with Michael is totally unexpected. I'm in my office going through the mail, and I slit an envelope open and pull out a handwritten letter. "Dear Kat, I've heard you several times on the radio talking about your organization's mission and would love to help." He goes on to share he's an architect doing his best to juggle the demands of his work with the challenges of single parenting his two kids. He lives in South Pasadena, which seems worlds away from Hemet. I'm intrigued and concoct a plan for him to come out and advise us on renovating one of our facilities.

I couldn't wait. We seem to have so much in common. I am hopeful this will end my losing streak on the dating front. The day comes for us to meet. Michael couldn't have been more gracious, but the chemistry wasn't there. He is the nicest guy ever, but I realize he isn't my type. I never expect anything more to come of it. But God has other plans.

Three months later, the phone rings. "Hi, this is Michael. I have no idea why I'm calling, but Friday night, I got this strange knock, knock from God to call you. I tried to ignore it, but He kept knocking. What's going on in your life?" I realize I have nothing to lose, and I unload on him. "Friday night, I was in a horrible accident that totaled my car. While sirens blared during my ambulance ride to the ER, I realized I had no one to call when something like this happened. Even the support group I go to is a bust. All they want to do is whine and complain. None of them want to play ball. And last week, Vanessa's social worker called to say there's an issue with the adoption now that I'm a single mom. What the bleep! Vanessa's parents abandoned her when she was diagnosed with a terminal brain tumor. Who else would take her? Let's face it, me being a single parent is the least of their worries. Then there's my son, Jeff. He's totally out of control. I've tried everything. I have no idea what else to do!"

I finally take a breath. Instead of an abrupt click on the other end of the line, I hear, "Wow, now I know why I called. Can I call you tomorrow?" Yeah, like that will ever happen. But it does. The next night and every night for a year, he called me. It is literally a lifeline and turns into a deep friendship.

After a year of late-night calls, Michael shows up at my door with a Golden Retriever and a bag of groceries. He says, "Relax and let me take over." What happens next is like something from one of those heartwarming Hallmark movies. Michael and Vanessa are on the kitchen floor, and the Golden is cuddling with Vanessa. Michael is pulling each ingredient out of the bag like magic. And it is. I am mesmerized as he shows Vanessa how to put it all together to make spaghetti. Her angelic smile permeates the room, reminding me how she stole my heart a year and a half earlier. I see Michael through new eyes, wondering if—okay, secretly hoping—this will lead to something more. Maybe the fact that he's not my type is a good thing. After all, my type didn't work out so well before.

Then it happens—an unexpected meltdown kiss that changes everything. In an instant, we go from friends to much more.

Now back to the bouquet and the baseball. I carefully remove the baseball and realize it's hinged. I open it up and see Michael has scooped out one side and placed a ring in it. The other side has a note that harkens back to something I said in that awful rant. It says, "Do you want to play ball?" How could I say no? It's been twenty-nine glorious years full of romance and amazing adventures with an incredible husband who became a wonderful father to Vanessa.

Saying "Yes" to Vanessa, and then Michael transforms my life and fills it with love, joy, laughter, and yes, some sadness.

Vanessa was an angel in our midst. Along her journey, she reflected God's enduring love, compassion, and grace in a way only she could.

In the aftermath of her cancer and related treatments, Vanessa has many cognitive, emotional, and physical challenges, but she never lets them get in the way of a life well-lived. Vanessa volunteered at the Pasadena Humane Society for over twelve years, caring for unadoptable animals. She worked part-time at PetSmart for ten years until her health declined to the point where she forgot to close the cages. Rats ran rampant, putting an end to that chapter.

While people would say I am her angel, she was my angel . . . a true gift from God. She taught me so much about what it means to be alive, to live in the moment with joy and hope, and to embrace gratitude even in unthinkable circumstances.

The doctor's prognosis of three months turns into twenty-six years. Twenty-six years of learning to be her mom and an endless advocate, ensuring she never becomes invisible to the doctors, educators, and other providers who help me care for her. I'm sure there were moments when they thought I was the mother from hell and, at other times, heaven-sent.

Vanessa's health continued to decline unmercifully, and I felt helpless. For the next five years, I struggle with anticipatory grief. Depression wove itself in and out of my denial, anger, and bargaining. Lots of bargaining. Acceptance felt elusive until Valentine's Day in 2015.

Twenty-six years after her diagnosis, Vanessa joins many of her friends for a tea party in heaven, including Mikey, who passed away just months after I took Vanessa home. The timing of her passing feels providential. Valentine's is the ultimate day of love. Her work on earth is done, and we have the privilege of ushering her back into the arms of God.

And there it is, the answer to "Why me, God?"

Vanessa is finally at peace. While she isn't cured, she is healed, and so am I.

I often wonder, what if I hadn't answered that unexpected 'call?'

Jennifer Thietz

https://www.linkedin.com/in/jenniferthietz
https://www.facebook.com/jennifer.thietz

Jennifer Thietz (nee Marais) RN, BSN, OCN, MSN obtained her Associate of Nursing Degree in South Africa in 1988 at the age of 21. She has years of experience working with patients in diverse settings in South Africa and the USA. She has a Bachelor of Nursing and a Master of Nursing Degree through an international distance learning program at the University of Dundee in Scotland. She has written a book for cancer patients and caregivers which has been distributed by a large pharmaceutical company in the USA.

Jennifer is tri-cultural having called Zimbabwe, South Africa, and the USA, home. Her heart now lies with the plight of nurses where she is focusing her considerable years of nursing experience, including her time working during the COVID pandemic, to address issues like compassion fatigue and burnout in nurses. She believes the time has come to empower and heal our nurses.

TRIBE OF ANGELS: LESSONS LEARNED ON RESILIENCE FROM NURSES DURING THE COVID PANDEMIC

By Jennifer Thietz

In March 2020, the thunder of pots and pans overtook Europe. People stood at open windows or on their balconies amid pot plants yearning for Spring with tears rolling down their faces. They banged and thumped with spoons and hammers, denting and cracking their pots as they tried to draw thunder out of them. But even this blast they created was not enough because their hearts were bursting. They needed each other, but this was different. They could not come together like they normally would cheer on their heroes amid war, flood, or fire because of this new, invisible enemy they could not see called COVID, which kept them apart. The barrage boomed up to the mountains and collided and ricocheted off stone walls and streets. Luckily, in early 2020, none of us knew the extent of the terror and suffering ahead of us.

I stood and watched those people banging for me and my Tribe of nurses on TV, and like them, I cried too. I was desperate and deeply touched—feelings I could not explain. I knew I was a fraud for being called a hero because there was nothing even remotely heroic or brave about me standing there crying in anticipation of what was to come. I was engulfed in fear by the arrival of the Pandemic.

Looking back, the thunder felt like a premonition that we were at war and our world as we knew it was about to end. The pandemic would stretch nurses from around the world to their breaking point, and I was one of them, many would lose their lives in the fight. The rest would walk through the fire, some becoming the walking wounded. Others would flee within a short time of that thunder, and those who were left behind would continue to fight. Surprisingly, some nurses could even thrive, coming out stronger and more beautiful in every way because of their resilience. How did they survive and flourish when so many other nurses would be forced to leave the profession, crippled by compassion fatigue and burnout?

I have been an RN for over 30 years, and back then, I worked as an oncology nurse navigator in a 400-bed hospital in Northern California. I left nursing in April 2022, just over two years after the Pandemic began, not because I was due to retire but because I had burnout. This was something I was sure would never happen. In 1988 as a 21-year-old RN in South Africa, I fell in love with nursing. It gave my life meaning, and it gave me the privilege of caring for extraordinary people along the journey. My career even brought me and my family across the world from South Africa to California. I never imagined I would end up leaving this job I loved and identified so strongly with, because I could no longer do it.

As the months ticked by in 2020, the world experienced shortages in protective clothing and medical supplies that impacted many nurses, increasing their risk of infection from COVID. At the same time, a dismal acceptance settled that not only older patients with other health problems were getting sick and passing away, but now young, supposedly healthy patients with no apparent health problems were joining them. People started to panic. At one point, one of our ICUs had four patients on ventilators due to COVID ranging in age from 21 to 42. We could not imagine what those nurses were going through as they witnessed the suffering of those young people and their loved ones. They cried for their patients, and when they saw what it was doing to their colleagues, they cried for each other too.

My Tribe was changing as they warred against the increasing uncertainty of a chaotic workplace running short on staff and supplies. It was as if these strong, energetic men and women I knew well and had worked with for years suddenly started to shrink, literally becoming smaller right in front of me. Constant frustration mixed with fear and, at times, the defeat left a strange empty look that none of us had seen in each other before. We knew the risks we were taking. We imagined what it might be like to be that nurse, struggling to breathe in that ICU bed, maybe even on a ventilator, because of many of the situations we were exposed to at work that we had no control over. Resilience was being called for on all fronts every time we walked through those hospital doors. I noticed more and more that those nurses who were building resilience together were more successful than those battling on their own.

Resilience is a skill that can be learned:

I thought being a Registered Nurse for over 30 years had given me the experience and resilience to survive the Pandemic. I had worked in Africa in various nursing roles that called for flexibility (including working in a Hospice where we tried to help our patients dying in shacks without water or electricity), but despite that, I found I was ill-prepared for this Pandemic.

It was deeply comforting to learn that resiliency is a skill that can be learned. Some can learn it more quickly than others, but all of us can become resilient in the face of challenges and trauma. This profound truth means that, although we are still reeling from the effects of a global Pandemic, there is a way forward. We can decide to be resilient and successful because we are prepared to learn how to.

Resilience is better when learned together:

Resilience in nursing is a word we hear daily. I have heard it described as the ability to withstand stress, recover quickly, and hang tough, as they say. The talent to be like an elastic band with the capability to spring back into shape when the crisis is over. But this crisis didn't end;

it just got worse and worse. The younger nurses, despite their lack of experience in the trenches, taught me more about the importance of togetherness in building resilience than I thought possible.

My daughter is also an RN and was in her late twenties at the time. She loved nursing. Early in 2020, she was working in acute care and nursing a baby at home simultaneously. One of her close nursing friends was also nursing a baby and worked with her in the same unit. They took all the precautions they could, knowing there was always the chance they were carrying the virus home to their babies. They poured their hearts out to each other, sharing their deepest fears and greatest triumphs while performing one of the world's hardest jobs in the world. They understood each other as no one else could. Their friendship grounded them no matter how bleak the circumstance. Their support of each other enabled them to overcome challenges and grow more resilient together.

Resilience grows when a decision is made, and action follows that decision:

I remember hearing about one of the ER doctors who camped in a tent in her yard so she would not bring the virus home to her husband and children. Her family would watch her through their window during the heat and cold of the day, like a nomad on a pilgrimage, and far from home in every respect apart from distance; she alienated herself from her loved ones to protect them. Another nurse left home for months and stayed with her mother so she wouldn't be around her children. They were too small to understand why she had suddenly dropped out of their lives and blamed themselves and their siblings. "Have I done something wrong? Does Mama not love us anymore?" they would ask her. Their mother called them every day to try and comfort them, and hearing the pain and accusations in her children's voices, she would cry every time she put down the phone because she knew they would remember what she had done, and no child should ever be pulled from the arms of their mother, especially at a time when everything they knew had changed.

Despite all this, these two women decided to sacrifice to save their family from the risk of COVID infection. They were unwavering in their decision. Some people disagreed with them, but they were unmoved; they had the self-confidence to decide on a plan that gave them peace and enabled them to place their energy where the world needed it. They understood indecision creates worry and dread if left too long, so they pulled the trigger and followed their plan.

Having a purpose in life helps build resilience:

Nurses worldwide continued to come to work no matter how grim the circumstance. They came for their patients because they knew it was the right thing to do. I watched my Tribe reaching forward to listen to the whispers and moans of their patients, some patients who were terrified of dying, and many utterly alone. Their nurses showed up, Angels covered in rigid masks and suits like warriors, holding hands that clutched onto them in that sacred moment, sharing the deepest part of their hearts at a time when the world shattered, and nothing was as it should have been.

Resilience grows when clear boundaries are in place:

Some patients and caregivers were very angry with the medical world, and many had every reason to be. They were alone and cut off. Many could not contact providers or offices, and when they did, they were not helped. The human connection so badly needed during this nightmare was cut off with little mercy. Anxiety seeped into everything, and medical providers found themselves at the mercy of angry patients and caregivers for things out of their control. It was difficult for them not to take it personally. Nurses were often caught in the crosshairs because, at times, they could not help either, or the little they managed to help was not enough, and both they and their patients knew it. The saddest thing was when the priceless gift of trust between a patient and their nurse was broken, not by the nurse, but by a sick and failing health system.

It was a time when strong boundaries were called for. Those nurses who managed to maintain intact boundaries were the ones who did not let themselves become overwhelmed and powerless in the face of guilt and offense. They could respond kindly but firmly to behavior that was not appropriate. They could apologize even if they were not to blame because they knew it was about the patient and not them. Their self-worth was intact when many colleagues second-guessed themselves and their roles. They demonstrated how creating and protecting their boundaries was necessary for resilience. How did they do that? They sharpened their ability to say no when needed. They listened to their needs and acted on those by moving away from uncomfortable situations. Their behavior was congruent with their beliefs.

Resilience is reflected in behavior:

Some nurses I knew responded entirely differently to the Pandemic from what I expected. A few isolated themselves and hid behind masks and goggles when they were the ones who had been the experts before the Pandemic. They drained their colleagues by being angry and negative, and they made little effort to reach out. On the other hand, those nurses who showed more resilience were the ones who kept communicating despite their difficulties. They were not afraid to voice their true feelings but not at the expense of others. They were comfortable being vulnerable and openly shared when they succeeded or failed so others felt comfortable being real with them.

Building resilience is a process requiring a change:

As I watched my Tribe of Angels, I saw them dig deep and begin a process in stages. It was not an organized process; the chaos continued.

Rachel Rogers

http://www.facebook.com/RachelJohnsonRogers
http://www.instagram.com/racheljohnsonrogers

Rachel is a mother, wife and former Skilled Nursing Facility Administrator. She has a passion working with the elderly and does consulting work with Dementia care.

She holds a bachelor's degree in Social Science with an emphasis in gerontology.

DELAYED GRIEF

By Rachel Rogers

My parents' love story began in the late 1960s. They met each other in Boston, Massachusetts in a church choir. Ruth and Robert Johnson had a lot of the same interests and loved music. My mother had studied to become a Registered Nurse in Minnesota. When she graduated, her first nursing position out of school was in Taiwan, where she assisted an English physician in a small acute hospital. She committed to a three-year contract and was immersed in the culture, even learning the Taiwanese language. In the summer of 1966, she decided to take a nursing class in Boston and met my father at the local church, where she was asked to join the choir one Sunday. They dated during the summer until my mother returned to Taiwan to complete her nursing assignment in the fall season. For the next year, my parents wrote letters back and forth to each other. This was the day and age of the real snail mail, each letter taking weeks to arrive. In the letters, my mother would often ask my father, "How old are you?" and he would reply, "If I told you how old I am, you may stop writing to me." As it turned out, my father was 22 years older than my mother. The relationship blossomed, and they ended up getting married in September of 1968. She was 28 years old, and he was 50 years old. They would always say that age was just a number and their love was solid. They made Newton, Massachusetts their home and raised my brother and I there until 1990, when they retired in California.

It was my 30th year on this earth. My mom, dad, and husband Matt had all gathered for my birthday at their California home. When I entered their kitchen, the warm aroma of cumin, garlic, and onions filled the air. On the menu was one of my favorite meals, lamb curry over white rice. The dish's toppings of coconut flakes, raisins, and peanuts were all ready to go on the decorated table. Her kitchen table was set with colorful birthday napkins and a plate at my setting that said, "It's your special day!" On the counter was a double-layer chocolate cake with chocolate frosting. I noticed that she had put in the trick candles that reignite after blowing them out; my mom loved a good joke. This was a tradition, as she had been preparing my favorite meal for me since I was ten years old. My parents were always so good about celebrating my birthday and truly made it a special day for me. They were a dynamic duo, my mom loved to cook and bake for anyone in the family celebrating a birthday, and my dad always had a great story to tell. I felt loved and secure in my family unit. Matt and I had been married for five years. Both of us were in our chosen careers and working up the ladder. All was well, or at least I thought so.

The year that I turned 30, my father, who was then 84 years old, suffered a major stroke. He had lost the ability to move the right side of his body and could not swallow well. After I visited with him at the hospital, I made my way to the lobby and called a friend to share the news. I could not believe how his physical state had changed so quickly from the funny storyteller I knew and loved to the fragile old man who had difficulty speaking. I cried the deepest cry to my friend, hardly catching my breath because I knew everything had changed. I knew I would never see his blue eyes again and hear his hearty laugh; I would never see that look in his eyes that told me he loved me with his whole heart. Within six weeks of the stroke, he declined dramatically and was terminal. We signed him up for hospice care and moved him into a private hospice home with nurses (angels) on duty 24/7. He was there for about ten days before he started to actively pass.

One evening I double-parked my car to rush into the hospice home to see him after work. At this point, his eyes remained closed, and he appeared to not even know anyone was present. I sat down and started talking to him. I thanked him for raising us in Boston, telling him that I enjoyed all the historical things we did there, like throwing tea in the

Boston harbor or watching the Boston Pops symphony play. I told him that moving to California was a great decision, as I found my life partner and loved the sunshine. At this point, the nurse came in and requested that I move my car because I was blocking someone. I got up to leave and told him, "I love you Dad." To our surprise, he replied, "I love you too!" It was the last words I heard him say. On the day he passed, I can remember sitting with my mother and witnessing him take his last breath. My sweet father was gone. I could have broken down and cried the days after his death. I could have felt the empty feelings and then the fondness of the great memories of him in my childhood and life. But I didn't. Without me really knowing it, I hit "pause" on the grief experience. We all handle grief differently, that's for sure. As for me, I held down the "pause" button for many years.

On the day he passed away, I drove my mother home to her house. Their home had a different energy now with my dad gone. There was no music playing, no sound of him yelling "Robert's home" when he walked in the front door, no compliments from him to my mother for a great meal. It was silent in a new way. I was determined to help my mother ease into this new world. I remember sleeping in the same bed with her the first couple of nights because I did not want her to feel alone. My new role had begun. I was my mother's "partner" now. For the next six months, I helped her with all the funeral arrangements, managing her household bills, helping her sell her home and find a new one, packed up all of their belongings, and moved her into a senior community for active seniors. I was the one that brought his wedding tuxedo to the funeral home for him to be cremated in it. My mother was not able to bring herself to do this task. She was 62 years old. The next year I became pregnant with my first child. Being busy and managing my mother's life helped me cope with the great loss we all felt.

At his funeral and in the years to come, I did not cry like I did that night in the hospital. I missed him immensely, but I would just zip up my emotions in a bag and put it on a shelf to deal with later. My focus for the years to come was on my mother's well being, my marriage, my job, and my new babies. The ball of grief was definitely there in my gut and heart. I could feel that my family structure was now different. My father's presence always made me feel stable and loved. I missed his great stories, and I missed watching him lay on the floor in front of his stereo and listen to Mozart, Louis Armstrong, and Bob Marley. I wanted to see him sitting in his chair reading the latest The New Yorker magazine. But there was no time to wallow, and I chose not to. It hurt too bad. I had decided to push forward and hold all of my emotions in. Keeping myself busy was the answer to not feeling the emotions of grief.

My mother knew as a young bride marrying an older man that she may be alone one day. She truly cherished her 34 years of marriage with my father. She was now a grandmother and loved helping me care for my two daughters. This was how she coped with the loss of her life partner. She continued to make family birthday celebrations a memorable event. After my father passed, she honored him by making his birthday meal, a pastie filled with steak and potatoes, and of course, his favorite dessert, a banana cream pie. My daughters loved eating her pies and would ask my mother about her husband that, in their child's minds, had "flown away" with the angels. My daughters did not have a chance to meet him. He would have been an amazing grandfather! It made me sad that he was not in their lives, but I kept those deep cries and sad feelings on the shelf. Then one night, nearly ten years after he passed, I heard a particular Bob Marley song that he used to play loud on his stereo to help wake up my brother and I when we were in high school. The thought of him playing a reggae song to lighten the mood in the house in the morning made me chuckle. I was now a mother and could understand more why setting the tone for kids' mood was a good idea. But that chuckle soon led to a deep cry. I found myself bawling on the sofa into a pillow. The rush of sadness took over me, and I felt like I had let out an enormous wave of grief that had been "paused" before. I was finally allowing myself to start the grieving process for my Dad.

During the next year, I cried more and loved to hear stories from my mother about their married life together. It felt good to feel the grief and begin to heal, but a new issue arose. My beloved mother was diagnosed with cancer. She had a cancerous soft tissue sarcoma in her leg that had seeded into her lungs. My immediate family opened our hearts and arms to my mother. While she was receiving treatment for her cancer, she continued to make sure that she acknowledged birthdays in our family with a meal and dessert., even pulling out the trick candles for a good laugh. She loved being a grandmother and poured herself into this role. It was her way of healing after my father passed. For years she was our number one babysitter and was very close with my daughters. Her new diagnosis was not going to slow her down, she thought, and she joined in on all the family events as usual. She tried to fight cancer with all she had, but in the end, the cancer won. Her health declined rapidly, and here I was again, signing up a parent for hospice care. She fought death in a big way. I witnessed her go through the stages of death: denial, anger, etc. She wanted to watch her grandchildren graduate from high school and enter the world. A few days prior to my mom's death, she asked me directly when my father was coming back. She said that he visited with her that morning. I knew the end was near and was glad to hear that my father, her love, would be there for her as she transitioned. My mother passed away two days after my 44th birthday. There was no homemade lamb curry or chocolate cake for this birthday. Instead, I got her looking directly into my eyes and holding my hands from her hospital bed. She could only speak a little bit, and she kept grabbing my cheeks and saying my name over and over. My brother and I were at her bedside when she took her last breath. I can say that for both of my parents, I witnessed their last exhale.

I was now an orphan. Both of my parents were gone. I did not want to press "pause" on my grief this time. I knew that, for me, deciding to hold back my feelings just made the whole experience much harder. I now had two daughters who absolutely adored their grandmother, and this was their first experience with death and loss. So I decided that I was going to "exhale" and feel the pains of grief. I had lost both of my parents this time. There were many tears and hard days. At times I felt overwhelmed with the thought that maybe I could have done more to prevent their passing, or at least make it easier to transition. But that was out of my control. For the first time in my life, I got a therapist to assist me with my anxiety and depression. In addition, I started doing yoga and meditation to help ground me. It's been six years now since my mother passed away. Some days are harder than others, but I feel a little lighter because I allowed myself to grieve her and my father's death. I would not say that I do not have hard days where I miss my family unit. My current birthdays are wonderful, but I do miss the taste of my mother's homemade meals and trick candles. Both of my parents live on in me and forever will. What I have learned about grief is that even if you put it on a shelf to deal with later, someday your "later" will come.

Monica M Marrone

Eco-wellness LLC
Health and Business Coach

https://www.linkedin.com/in/monicamarrone/
https://www.facebook.com/monica.marrone1
https://www.instagram.com/livingyoungerlonger
https://www.monicamarrone.com
http://ecowellnessllc.com/

Monica Marrone is a health and business coach. Her mission is to inspire you to become your healthiest self so you can best serve God and others. Her aim in sharing her story of fidelity in marriage and perseverance in the face of challenges is to encourage you to overcome whatever trials come your way.

Her chapter in You Can You Will is titled Miracle Moments, and it chronicles how God's grace held her family together through the dark chapters of co-dependency, addiction, and mental illness. It's a story of faith and forgiveness conquering fear and despair. Her mission is to overcome this generational cycle for her family and inspire others to do the same.

Monica worked for 25 years as a graphic artist. Now she pours her creative energy into her holistic approach to health: Living Younger Longer.

Growing up in an Italian home, she developed a love for preparing and sharing meals with friends and family. This passion for food and hospitality is a part of her recipe for healthy living. For the full, flavorful experience, you need all five ingredients: food, faith, fitness, friendship, and finance.

Her motto is to Be More, Make More, and Give More!

She lives in WI with her husband.

MIRACLE MOMENTS

By Monica M Marrone

Dedicated to Eric, who still suffers.

I always planned to get married in the church, but I didn't plan to fall in love with a divorced man who wasn't Catholic. My family loved Derrick's gregarious personality until I announced that I was moving to Texas and we would be married... at some future date. I vividly remember the round of phone calls with hysterical pleas from my mother and interrogations from my brothers imploring me to come to my senses.

We accelerated the wedding date, Derrick went through the process to join the Catholic Church, and we found out that his previous marriage was not an obstacle. Remarkably, my family had a change of heart and rallied to help me plan and organize a joy-filled celebration.

His voice was quivering as he stood at the podium. "...bearing with one another and forgiving one another, if one has a grievance against another; as the Lord has forgiven you, so must you also do. And over all these put on love, that is, the bond of perfection..."

The tears welled up in my eyes as I heard the words of the second scripture reading spoken by my Father on my wedding day. I was his only daughter, his youngest child of four, and the first to be married.

The intimate chapel was packed with my closest friends and family, and the tears kept flowing down my cheeks (and most of the congregation's) as the ceremony progressed. This covenant relationship I was entering into with my husband Derrick was the culmination of my faith journey. This Miracle Moment of our sacramental marital bond was the foundation that held us together through the storms that lie ahead.

"I'm sorry Derrick, you have to leave. You can't stay here anymore!" Seven years had passed. Although I knew I was making the "tough love" decision I needed to make, it was one of the most challenging days of my life. I still loved my husband deeply, but couldn't live with him any longer. The broken promises, the erratic behavior, and the rounds of in-patient and outpatient rehab led us to this fateful day. I stood by the window, watching him walk away. He had nothing, no job, no car, no friends, no money, and nowhere to go.

My heart ached as both the delightful and despairing memories flooded back through my mind.

I recalled our favorite courting memory when we were snuggling on the couch in my apartment. We were so in love. I thought, "I don't want to be anywhere else in the world than right here on this couch with you." I felt totally accepted and loved in a way I had never experienced before. Over the years, I realized that I had not fully reciprocated this complete acceptance of Derrick. I had seen his wild side when we were dating but fooled myself into thinking he would settle down after we married. My pride led me to believe that I was a "good influence" and could somehow mold him into the stable, attentive husband I so desired.

That first year of married life in Texas marked one of the darkest 12 months of my life. The bliss of the wedding day evaporated into loneliness, mistrust, deception, and chaos. The insecurity from being away from my friends and family led me to lean on Derrick for all my emotional support, and the more I clung to him, the more he ran away. I remember late nights feeling abandoned in our rental home, staring at the TV to numb the worry about where Derrick was and what he was doing. Money was rapidly disappearing from our checking account, and his behavior became increasingly erratic. Everything came to a head when he lost his job. Finally, Derrick fessed up that he was addicted to meth and promised me it would stop.

A promise that he was not capable of fulfilling.

How did we go from the joy of our wedding day to this nightmare in one year? I was terrified to tell my family the truth about what was happening because of their initial opposition to our wedding. And then I realized that this pattern of abandonment, addiction, and financial problems was not just my story; but a generational one.

I promised myself I would not marry someone like my father, but that was exactly what I did. Although my dad had some of the same character traits that attracted me to Derrick: outgoing, creative, imaginative, sentimental, and a bit of a dreamer, he also had many of the same flaws. My dad was often unreliable, unstable, unemployable, rebellious, and suffered from addictions.

The feeling of abandonment in my marriage often brought back memories of my childhood. "Wait here, Mon; I'll return in a few minutes." My Dad said, instructing me to wait in the car. We were in a strange neighborhood in Chicago. It was a busy street lined with businesses, bars, and restaurants. A few minutes passed, and anxiety took hold in my eight-year-old heart and mind. "Why didn't he take me with him?" More time passed, and my thoughts magnified to frantic worry. I attempted to hide in the back seat so the strangers passing by couldn't see me. "What if something happened to him? Each minute that passed seemed like 10 in my young mind. When he finally returned to find me in tears, he brushed it off without validating my feelings and fears. Years later, I realized he probably stopped to visit his bookie and stayed for a couple of drinks.

Derrick and I managed to find our way back to Chicago from Texas and pieced together some happy times, but the pattern of addiction and broken promises continued. Almost everyone in my life (including my therapist) encouraged me to get divorced. Yet, my heart always led me back to our wedding day and the belief that the Holy Spirit had blessed our bond. I chose to live alone but never felt compelled to divorce. I'm convinced God's grace gave me the courage to deliver the ultimatum to Derrick the day I watched him walk away from our apartment with no idea what he would do.

It turned into a Miracle Moment as he made the choice to walk 15 miles and check himself into a 30-day rehab program followed by a three-month stay in a psychiatric hospital. Derrick threw himself wholeheartedly into the hard work of healing from the mental and physical abuse he experienced as a child. 12-step programs were a critical part of his recovery, and we reconciled after a period of separation.

We moved to Madison, WI, for my job, and although Derrick was still struggling at times, we entered into a period of stability. My career in the graphic arts industry was growing, and Derrick worked part-time while returning to school and became an RN.

"It's a boy," was the good news I heard in the operating room on February 13, 1998. We were blessed with a child 15 years into our marriage. This joyful Miracle Moment would not have happened had I given up on my marriage during the stormy first chapter. I was elated and hopeful but also frustrated that I had to return to a full-time corporate job when David was only eight-weeks-old. The primary desires in my heart were more time with my family and to stay healthy so I could be active as David grew up. We were searching for ways to simplify our lives.

"Hey Mona, let's go look at this house." We weren't planning to move, but Derrick was so excited about the ad he found in the paper that I agreed to look. It wasn't our dream home, but it matched our goals of reducing our monthly expenses, resulting in a shorter commute for me, and providing an opportunity for me to cut back on my work hours. The abundant blessings of finding a Catholic faith community and dear friends that would be our safety net through the next dark chapter were not evident yet. The Holy Spirit was at the helm again, guiding Derrick to suggest this move and creating another Miracle Moment.

I was growing increasingly dissatisfied at work even though they paid me well. My interests had shifted to family life, faith life, and my part-time health and wellness business. When I lost my job in 2005, I was excited because I saw it as an opportunity to pursue my entrepreneurial passion. On the other hand, Derrick was riddled with fear of financial problems (I was the primary income earner) and angry that I refused to get another job in my field. This conflict between us only deepened in the years to come as one challenge after another came our way. Derrick had a series of surgeries culminating with a spinal fusion in 2006 that ultimately marked the loss of his career as an RN, chronic pain, depression, and addiction to narcotic pain meds.

After almost 12 years of sobriety and stability, we were again adrift in a stormy sea that brought us to the brink of unraveling as a family more times than I can count. The cycle of addiction and crazy behavior was back, and this time it was even more painful because I could see its effect on our son during a formative time in his life. David and I grew to dread that moment when we would turn into the driveway and hit the garage door opener. Would he be home or disappeared on some unknown excursion? I vividly recall the endless nights praying at David's bedside for his Dad and having to tuck him in, trying my best to trust God that Derrick would eventually return home.

I cycled through fear, anxiety, anger, and despair. Sometimes all in one day. I was in a perpetual state of alert, wondering when the next catastrophe would arise. On top of the emotional crisis, we were in the midst of a financial one, too, having lost two incomes in less than two years.

The craziness came to a crescendo in 2009 when Derrick ran away to Hawaii. I vividly remember feeling like someone had yanked out my heart as I came to the realization that he was gone. The thought of facing David after school was more than I could bear. So I called one of my "church lady" friends, explained what had happened, and asked, "Can Dave go home with Ben after school?" This support network of families from our church was the gift God gave us to carry us through this challenging time. Their children were his best friends at school, and their homes provided him with positive experiences in contrast to the chaos and confusion of our household.

By the time Derrick contacted me and declared that he wasn't sure he was returning, I had already filed for divorce. Over the next seven weeks, we tried to hammer out the details. I turned to my faith in a way I hadn't in a long time. My search to trust God more completely led me to attend a spiritual healing conference in Chicago. On the Saturday evening during the event, I went to a very introspective place and thanked God for all that happened, as it forced me to rely on Him more deeply. I didn't pray that Derrick would return but that God would reveal the truth to him about our marriage.

On the drive home, my phone rang. "Monica, I don't know what happened, but you must have been praying up a storm. I realize I'm never going to find another woman that loves me as much as you do. I'm coming back." This is the most direct and immediate answer to a prayer that I have ever received and our ultimate family Miracle Moment.

By Wednesday of that week, Derrick was back in Wisconsin and working on finding balance for himself. Over the next few years, our lives started moving in a positive direction, but the road was still rocky, with many detours and pitfalls. We eventually were led to a psychiatrist who diagnosed Derrick with bipolar disorder. It was an eye-opening moment after more than 25 years of marriage. His behavior pattern was familiar to me as it was similar to my Dad's. And yet, I was so caught up in the craziness of surviving the day-to-day melodrama that I didn't push to have him evaluated even though I knew my Dad was diagnosed with bipolar disorder as an elderly man! Once Derrick started on the prescriptions for bipolar disorder, life started to normalize. He still has chronic pain from his surgeries, but has learned to cope without narcotics and has gradually gotten off many of the anti-depressant drugs he was on for years.

Looking back on the dark times, I realize that I numbed my feelings to survive the pain. I tucked my heart away in a box and locked it up for safekeeping. The first step toward healing was to find the key. Then I had to develop the willingness to open the box and be vulnerable again. The desire to trust and love has become more powerful than the tendency to shrink back in fear. I know this process is essential to become fully human and the woman God intended for me to be. I'm emerging from the shadows as a vibrant woman who embraces the people and the opportunities I encounter with energy, enthusiasm, and child-like wonder. All the experiences of my life, the delightful and the despairing, are being woven into an astonishing tapestry. Now I realize that I need every thread for the picture to be complete.

Overcoming the cycle of addiction, co-dependence, unforgiveness, and mental illness is a never-ending process. Many of life's lessons I had to learn over and over. I can't control other people or events, but I can be the master of my attitude. I can choose to love rather than blame. I can choose to forgive rather than hold onto anger and resentment. I need to do this for my sanity, but more importantly, so that I don't pass this cycle down to my son the way my parents passed it down to their family.

As Derrick and I approach our 40th wedding anniversary, gratitude often fills our hearts. We survived the chaos and confusion, the deception and despair. This crazy journey has made us strong. By sharing our story of hope, we can move out of survival mode into thriving. We can take the pain and turn it into a passion for helping others. On the top of our gratitude list is the healing that has taken place for David and his chosen path to join the seminary and prepare to become a Catholic priest.

The gift of one more Miracle Moment came as a letter from my son on Mother's Day 2021. "I am who I am largely because I learned how to think and act from you and because of the virtue you have. I am a holy and capable man who desires the truth and to do God's will. This is true because of you, not in spite of you. I thank God for blessing me with you, Mom, and for you trying your best to do His will."

Stacy Aslan

Stacy Aslan is a woman of faith who loves to encourage, share and embrace life's ups and downs with other women. Stacy is known for her TGIF messages that go out on Fridays that bring her readers blessings and tight hugs.

BLESSINGS AND TIGHT HUGS

By Stacy Aslan

Have you ever thought of your life as a butterfly?

I have loved butterflies since I was a little girl. I love the way they flutter around and are so delicate. They come in all rays of color and size. I didn't realize until recently that my life has been like a butterfly, not in the flutter around and delicate way but in the metamorphosis way. I heard of people who have lost a parent, but I never thought I would be "that" person. The person that would grow up without my birth father guiding me through life. The day I was told of my dad's death was life changing for my mother, sister, and me. I never thought that a little girl could become stronger in her existence at such a young age. I was a young girl that had to transform into being adult when my dad passed tragically. I will never forget that day back on October 31,1975. I was an eight-year-old child,a daughter, and a big sister. I was way too young to take on the responsibilities that some requested of me, but I did because I was told, "You are the big sis, so you'll need to be there to help your mom, and you'll need to be a good example for your little sister," who was five years old at the time.

Throughout my life, I will never forget those words and those expectations. It wasn't until later in life that I realized this is where my transformation began. I loved my dad, and I have faint memories of him tucked away in my heart. My mom loved taking pictures, so I'm very thankful to her for capturing our short lifespan together as a family. My mom was the rock. She always made things out to be okay. I don't think she ever knew of the pressure placed on me by the words of someone just trying to be helpful and encouraging. They didn't know that I would take their words to heart and turn them into living actions. Observing the life cycle of the butterfly in and of itself holds rich symbolism and meaning.

Different Native American tribes interpret butterflies in their own way, but generally, they're thought to represent change and transformation, comfort, hope, and positivity. While some believed ancestors communicated through butterflies, others took the presence of these creatures as a joyous or hopeful sign. What I didn't know was that butterflies have a short lifespan, but through that short lifespan they go through a metamorphosis stage. Metamorphosis means to transform into something. My life had been transformed by such words that I took and put into actions, and by life's circumstances that I didn't choose but were chosen for me.

When I look back now, I'm thankful for my grandmother, my dad's mom, because she would share stories about my dad with me and tell me that one day, I'd get to see my dad again in heaven. That's where my Christian walkway back as a little girl began because I would not miss out on seeing my dad. I wasn't really raised in a church-going family, but I was raised in a believing household by my mom, who gave me the option of attending church and participating in whatever religion I chose. My mom's grandma, my great grandma, would take my sister and I to her church occasionally on Sundays, where we would get to attend Sunday school. remember those days now as seed planters in my faith walk because, over the years, I have been transformed.

Isaiah 41:10 - So do not fear, for I am with you, do not be dismayed, for I am your God. I will strengthen you and help you; I will uphold you with my righteous right hand. strengthen you and help you.

This verse became a lifeline for me to visually hold on to. When I say a lifeline, it's because if losing my dad at eight years old wasn't sad enough, when I was 25, my mom passed away from a heart attack at the age of 49. When my dad died, I had my mom, who allowed me to grieve on my own terms as far as going to the cemetery or celebrating or not celebrating my dad throughout the years, but now I have no one as far as a parent to guide me through such grief. I'm thankful that God has planted beautiful mentors in my life at just the right times when he knew I'd need them. My aunt Kathy was one of them who would be there and reassure me that God sees my broken heart, and that he loves me and will see me through it. Then I would reflect again on the verse 41:10 - So do not fear, for I am with you, do not be dismayed, for I am your God. I will strengthen you and help you; I will uphold you with my righteous right hand.

I believe that is why I'm strong today. I'm a lover, not a fighter, but I do have the will to fight and not give up. I may not have my dad or mom here to go to, but I do have my heavenly father, who will see me through by extending his right hand to me. His right hand that I grasp tightly and will not take for granted. Life is a gift he gives us as a present to unwrap daily, so why not make the best of it?

One time at a woman's Christian retreat after my mom had passed, I was watching a mother and daughter laughing and communicating in such a special way that I felt this lump of sadness and jealousy come over me. As I'm watching them, I'm struggling with the 'if only' feeling. So, being a Christian who knows that being jealous of something or someone isn't right, I went to the prayer room they had set up and asked for prayer over my situation. The young woman in her early 20s prayed with me this prayer: please Lord, fill Stacy's heart with love and joy whenever she sees a situation that makes her heart sad, that is camouflaged in jealousy. Be there with her and help her embrace it as a blessing. Amen.

As I sat there taking it all in, I asked her, "Can I pray for you?" And she said, "Yes, please pray that when I see a young mom pushing a baby stroller or playing on a playground that I don't feel jealous or sad because I won't be able to have children." We made a pact on that day so that whenever one of us felt sad or jealous in the situation, regardless of where we were, we'd pray for each other.

My prayer partner passed away a few months later due to a brain tumor. Even though she passed, I knew my way to carry on our pact was to pray the same prayer with other women that needed a prayer partner. Change, even through death, gives us the opportunity to grow even if we don't like it. It invites us to look at the inner self that is being transformed to become stronger and empower us to be the extraordinary person God created.

As I reflect on the other things in my life, a stepfather who loves me even though my mom has passed on, I celebrate 29 years of marriage that blessed me with two boys that I adore who are now young men, my sister who walks this journey with, me yet has her own story to tell and all my family and friends. I have grown to acknowledge that I do have a purpose in life. A purpose of sharing my life experiences in hopes of allowing someone not to feel alone. In hopes of allowing a young child who just lost a parent not to take on such burdens of being told to be the big sis or brother at such a young age. But to walk alongside that child and be an encourager and to take that pressure from them so they can become the most beautiful butterfly God is creating them to be. I don't want just to share my story. I want to be alive in my story to give everyone a chance to walk in my shoes, room to feel the emotions, and not be controlled or trapped in them. I want to embrace it and learn from situations that lead me to be a better person in life. The life that God is allowing me to take a deep breath in and exhale so that others can have the same opportunity and come out of that metamorphosis stage to thrive. No matter how long of a lifespan they have, it's worth living and enjoying it to the fullest, so the transformation will be looked at over time as the most beautiful part of life. When I asked family and friends what is something they remember about my dad and mom? I have been told that my dad gave the best tight hugs not tight like a bear hug but would linger on as in you knew you knew you were loved. When your mom would laugh it was contagious and everyone enjoyed her sense of humor. What is a trait that you would like or love to be remembered by? I feel that God uses life experiences for us to walk beside others some believers and some may still be searching. May your faith outweigh your fear. Psalms 91:4 - He will cover you with his feathers. He will shelter you with his wings. His faithful promises are your armor and protection. This is my signature verse because the Lord has given me feathers in my life when I really needed them to confirm what was written so long ago is still true today. It's okay not to know everything, as long as you have faith. and It's not too late to be transformed.

God is Good All The Time
Blessing and Tight Hugs
Stacy

Sharon Williams

MFT, MPA

http://linkedin.com/in/sharon-williams-1a175035

I am a proud mom of 3, grandmother to 6. and serial entrepreneur. Currently, I have a full time practice as a Marriage and Family Therapist. I have been a business woman with experiences ranging from owning my own flower shop to working in public television, running day care centers, to advocating for children's issues. I was on faculty in the community college arena for 17 years. Most importantly, my work to help children is my legacy.

IT'S THE HEARTBEAT

By Sharon Williams

All around the world, from sea to sea, from the beginning of life as we know it, there has been a heartbeat to a living thing. Give or take a little, the human heartbeat everywhere is approximately 84 beats a minute. If we are very quiet, we can actually hear another's heartbeat if we are very close to their heart. We can even feel another's heartbeat at various points on the body. We take the heartbeat for granted. After all, it just beats!

The smallest animal in the world is a pygmy shrew, weighing one ounce. The pygmy shrew's heartbeat is 1200 beats a minute.[1] Google says that the Wild Blue Whale's heartbeat, when diving for food, has two beats per minute. A giraffe has three hearts and other mammals could have up to 10 hearts. Yet, humans have somewhere around 84 beats a minute and one heart.

Imagine a human who is calm (approximately 84 beats a minute) holding a crying baby. If that human picks the baby up with a calm heartbeat and holds the baby close to his heart, the baby will begin to calm and synchronize with the calm heartbeat. Humans are so intricately made that their pleasure and safety come from another being. A person learns to regulate themselves when they are around two years old. How does this come about?

According to Erik Erikson, an infant develops trust in his world by being fed when he is hungry, picked up when he cries, warmed when cold, and unwrapped when too hot. This continues until he is two.

---

[1] Liz Langley, "Small Wonder: What Are the World's Tiniest Animals?," Animals (National Geographic, March 20, 2015), https://www.nationalgeographic.com/animals/article/150320-animals-smallest-lemurs-sharks-bats-butterflies-science.

During this time he is building a powerful emotion called trust. He learns this as his caregiver is at his command for all his basic needs.

During this time, he has learned to scoot, crawl, walk, and roam safely. He begins to learn to leave his caregiver by 8 or 10 feet or without being able to see the caregiver for a noticeably short period of time. As soon as he realizes he may be alone, he goes in search of his caregiver to be filled up with some fuel in the form of hugs and reassurance that he is fine, and safety is nearby. He was alone, yet he learned he could be safe because his caregiver was nearby. Is it the heartbeat he seeks? He can then go back out to learn to become more self-sufficient. Slowly, very slowly, he wanders off to have more novel experiences.

This boy, or maybe girl, continues through other stages of development until one day, life comes to a screeching halt. Facing the boy is the most beautiful girl in the world. Every beat of his heart is filled with the image of her. His heart is absolutely at high speed when he is near her. The brain has engaged the heart in yet another way.

The amygdala, a tiny almond-shaped piece of the brain, takes charge. The information for this boy is "go." When he was a child, he was well taken care of and loved through all his stages with no disappointments. Seems safe.

The amygdala does not have a record of heartbreak. The boy moves forward. If the same boy had been raised with heartbreak and disappointment, he may very well dispose of these feelings. The amygdala may report "danger." The heartbreak may have advised him through his cortex, the executive area of his brain, and probably said "stay away." Humans are designed for pleasure, contentment, delight, and cloud nine. The executive order of the brain denies anything adverse. Desire may trump the advice of the cortex, but only danger may possibly await.

ANSWERING THE CALL LIGHT

By Janet Williams

Nurses are healthcare professionals who are at the forefront of patient care, dealing with various illnesses, injuries, and conditions. One of the most significant challenges that nurse face is the loss of patients. Losing patients is an inevitable part of a nurse's job, but it can be difficult to cope with the emotional toll it takes on them. Nurses are caring individuals who form close relationships with their patients, and seeing them suffer or pass away can be devastating.

As emergency nurses, we have patients that often use our services. They have conditions that need more attention than their primary care provider can manage. These individuals come to the department and spend many hours in our care while their conditions are stabilized. We become the lifeline for these people, and we build a bond that is hard to describe. We know each other by name, they know who established their IV last time, and they count on us to make them feel better. There are times when we are unable to reverse the years of disease that these patients have endured. On the days that we lose these patients, we experience a wide range of emotions, including sadness, guilt, anger, and frustration.

The most common emotion that nurses feel after losing a patient is sadness. We may have spent weeks, months, or even years caring for a patient and getting to know them and their families. In getting to know these families, we try to remember small things about them, such as information about their grandchildren, the name of their pet, or what happened to them during their last visit.

Nurses may feel a sense of guilt after a patient's passing, even if there was nothing they could have done to prevent it. They may feel like they could have done more or made different decisions that would have led to a better outcome. This guilt can be especially difficult to deal with if the patient's family blames the nurse or healthcare team for the death.

Nurses may also feel anger after losing a patient. There can be a sense of frustration with the healthcare system or even with the patient. In the times since Covid, the availability of resources to patients are harder to navigate. This can be difficult for the emergency nurse because patients have such complex problems that are difficult to address with a visit to the emergency department. The anger that is associated with a patient refusing to follow a treatment plan can be difficult. These patients have resources that they have chosen not to use to improve their health.

Nurses may feel frustrated after losing a patient because we may not understand why the patient passed away. We may feel like we did everything right and within our power but still couldn't save the patient's life. The frustration can be compounded by the fact that nurses often work with patients with chronic illnesses or life-threatening conditions.

Coping with the loss of patients can be challenging for nurses, but there are ways to help them through the grieving process. Nurses can benefit from talking to their colleagues, attending support groups or counseling sessions, or taking time off to grieve. Healthcare organizations can also provide resources and support to help nurses cope with patient loss.

One of the best ways for nurses to deal with the loss of patients is to talk to other colleagues. In the emergency department, we have a critical debriefing after the traumatic loss of a patient. We talk to each other about what brought the patient to the hospital, what we did right, and how we can support each other. The leader of this conversation will then follow up with the participants in a few days, a couple of weeks, and a month to make sure that the nurse is coping with the loss of the patient. Talking to others who have gone through similar experiences can be a great source of comfort and support.

Nurses can also benefit from attending support groups or counseling sessions. These groups provide a safe space for nurses to share their feelings and work through grief with trained professionals. Counseling can be especially helpful for nurses struggling with guilt, anger, or frustration.

Nurses may need to take time off to grieve after losing a patient. Taking a break from work can help them process their emotions and come to terms with the loss. Healthcare organizations should encourage nurses to take time off if they need it and provide paid leave if possible.

Healthcare organizations can also provide resources and support to help nurses cope with the loss of patients. This can include counseling services, debriefing sessions, and training on grief and loss. These resources can help nurses feel supported and valued, which can improve their emotional well-being and job satisfaction.

After my many years of caring for patients of all ages, some of the lessons I have learned are:

1. Garner support from your colleagues: There is something comforting about talking to a person who has walked in your shoes.
2. Practice Self-Care: While this may sound cliche, I have found it helpful to disconnect by finding activities I love, such as going to concerts, reading, taking a walk, or calling a friend. By addressing my emotional needs, I am able to process my emotions more fully.
3. Get Support: Whether that be through professional counseling, support groups, your pastor, or friends, releasing emotions and feelings is helpful for healing.

4. Reflect on your role: Understanding I provided the best care possible and that only God can control our death helps to remind me to rest in faith.

As a nurse, it has taken time for me to find outlets for the emotions and feelings I experience while at work. It isn't as easy as leaving the hospital as if nothing difficult happened - you can't forget the experiences you have as a clinician. I became a nurse to help others find health and wellness, so when a life is lost, it affects me greatly.

If you aren't a nurse, I encourage you to support caregivers as they diligently work to take care of you and your loved ones. The emotional toll each day is real. We care for each patient as if it were our loved one. Your health and comfort are our first concern - know when you come for treatment, YOU matter.

Helen Wuckowitsch

Empower Encourage
Encourager

https://www.linkedin.com/in/helen-wuckowitsch-03785b245/
https://www.facebook.com/helen.wuckowitsch
https://www.instagram.com/livingstonwuckowitsch
https://www.helenwuckowitsch.com

A Grandmother of 14, Encourager, Retired Business Owner, Caregiver, Photographer, and I work part time in an Attorney's office. All my life I was someone's daughter, mother, wife, employee, helper, you name it. Doing what I am told, not giving an opinion, going along with everyone and everything. I am now becoming who I am. NOW I am Helen. Daughter of the King, Uniquely Gifted, Redeemed, Sanctified, Set Free, Alive in Christ Jesus and I have something to say. I mentor several young women. I started two Facebook pages, 714 prayer and Empower Encourage. My favorite things to do are spend time with my 5-year-old Granddaughter when she spends 2 nights a week, to go kayaking, and visit my friends. I attend church on Sunday and a Filipino-American Bible Study every other Friday night. I am looking forward to each new day and all that God has planned for me.

POWER OF WORDS

By Helen Wuckowitsch

There is power of life or death in the very words you speak. As for me, the words spoken over me brought bondage, fear of speaking, thinking, even hoping, and depression over my life until, with God's help, I Broke Free.

'No one cares what you think, no one cares what you have to say, you are worthless , a liar, and no one will believe you.'

These were words spoken over me as a small child and occasionally by people I allowed into my life.

In the first years of life, my folks were indigent farmers, following the crops. We picked cotton, walnuts, oranges, grapes etc. We lived in the work camps in a one room shack with a shared bathroom/shower house. It was a terrifying place to live. When I was six, we lived in a big home on a mountain, the kids (there were five of us under 10 at that time, with a couple of teenage brothers) would have to take a nap, but I always had to sleep in a room all alone when everyone else got to sleep together in another room. I didn't understand. I was very scared. I was always told, 'Don't talk, just do as you are told. Nobody wants to hear anything you have to say, they won't believe you, you were made to please man.'

As I grew older, I was so excited as I thought of all the possibilities for my life. I was only 17, but I was finally getting something I had dreamed of: A baby of my own! Who I can love, and who will love me. Someone I could teach that "You are unique and amazing, you have a voice, hope, and a future, any life you can think or imagine. The world is yours for the taking." Having my firstborn son gave me hope for my future. Then a year later, my precious daughter was born. I'd decided on a name for my future daughter when I was 12. I prayed to God every moment that she would have a voice. (Be careful what you pray for). She was screaming as she came into this world, started talking full sentences when she was one, and definitely has a voice.

I'm sure you have had times when you thought, "This is it. I'm finally getting what I've wanted for so long." Then, when reality sets in, it is nothing like you had imagined. I married the father of my baby in a rushed wedding. I was so excited about what my future would be. By the time I was 19, I was having my third baby (Shari Lyn) who died right after she was born. We moved a lot during these years. Then it seemed like we were going to settle down; we were buying our dream home, settled in a community and a church, which we were very active in, and our future was bright. My son and my daughter were beautiful, amazing, intelligent, unique, and eager to learn individuals. It looked like my dreams were coming true. I would be a mother, a wife, involved in my church and my community, raise my children in the same home, play with my grandchildren in the home their parents were raised in, and I would live "happily ever after." Then that marriage ended after yet another broken promise. I had to choose myself! By doing that, I also chose my children. I was committed to building a life of stability for my family to give them what I didn't have. What a blow to my dream, my emotions, and my children. We had to start again, and the dream of building the "traditional" family was still alive. I knew this couldn't be the end.

I thought I had beaten the odds and showed those voices I heard over and over that they didn't know what they were saying. The next ten years were like going from heaven straight into the pits of hell.

The feelings I couldn't escape were to find a man to get love and approval.

This time, I married a man 40 years older than me. He had three beautiful children, a very young daughter, a son, and a daughter in their late teens. What a gift I was given to be in a place to speak life, love, and truth over them. My daughter-in-law and I became very close. I encouraged her, helping her to understand her value. She was in a volatile relationship. Through that time, I supported her in understanding she deserved to be treated with love and kindness. She got pregnant and had a baby. I supported her through it all, offering her words of wisdom from my experience. It was important she knew she had a voice that should be heard. As our friendship grew, we were able to talk about her value, her worth, and the innate ability she had to be the mother she dreamt of for her children. I was there for all of his daughters. I encouraged and protected them. And through that, I watched them become courageous! Oh, the joy of seeing young women use their words, know their value, and make choices in their best interest. I was beginning to understand the true power of words.

So here I was, helping other women find their voices and understand who they are. And I'm still not speaking up for myself. Why can't I speak up for myself? Why can't I use the power of my words for ME?

Then, I discovered that my stepson was having my very young teenage son sell drugs on the street.

I found the courage for my children, so I gathered them up to get them to safety. This time, I was committed to using my voice and making choices that would be good for me.

We got a new start, and for three years I devoted my time to recreating our life. But then, I found myself looking for love—looking for a man. I was insecure. I didn't have a voice. I didn't speak up. I didn't speak out. I got involved with another man and married him. He was verbally abusive. He made sure I understood I was to be seen and not heard and that there was nothing I had to say that he or anyone else wanted to hear. By this time, my son had graduated, moved out of the home, and was working. And my daughter, then just 16, moved in with her grandparents because she could not stand this man I married. And I didn't speak up for my children. I continued to listen, obey, and do as I was told. He even had our church family fooled.

How did I let this happen again?

Crying out to God, I accepted the mistreatment. I worked and gave all my money to him. I lost everything I had—everything I'd saved from my children growing up, all my baby pictures, and everything my children made me. Because I let him take over my life, I gave up my choices, my reality. I finally got the courage to leave when he took me by the throat and pushed me against the wall. Physical abuse was terrifying. I tried to kill myself three times during that marriage.

When I was almost 40, I was alone, feeling unloved, unwanted, undesirable, had nothing to say, intimidated, and holding on by a thread. Then my dearest friend introduced me to my current husband. He was kind and compassionate to me. We moved in together. The first three years were hard. I was a wreck from the verbal and physical abuse of my ex-husband, and from losing my children for not being there when they grew up and graduated. I was beating myself up, and now my husband got the brunt of all that. I would scream and yell and accuse him of everything. I was verbally abusive to him, and he would just pat me on the back and say it's going to be okay, you're going to be okay. And he did that for three years, Never defending himself or taking offense at what I was accusing him of. All that time, I was trying to speak up and find my voice. I was reading self-help. I was trying to find myself, find out who I am, and find my voice. I enrolled in college, and I was educating myself. We got married, then we started a photography business and worked all the time. After seven years, we started a restaurant business. Again we lived together and worked together seven days a week, grinding these businesses. Then I found out that I had Hashimoto's thyroid disease and was going through menopause. All the hormonal changes were going on, and life was exhausting. I still did not have my voice. I could not voice my opinions. I could not quiet the voices.

I spent a lot of time reading and studying self-help books, praying and reading the bible, and searching for the strength and courage to speak up. How do I speak out? Yes, I loved God and still went through everything I went through, still making one bad decision after another. I felt all alone, but I was never really alone. The Holy Spirit was always there, nipping at my heels. It took quite a while, but I found the courage. One bible verse really helped me through these hard days:

Lamentations 3:21-24
Yet this I call to mind
And therefore I have hope.
It is of the Lord's mercies
That we are not consumed
Because His compassions fail not
They are new every morning
Great is thy faithfulness
The Lord is my portion
Saith my soul
Therefore I will have Hope in Him

Finally, I just cried out and said, "Okay, that's it. I'm just going to get a divorce. I'm done with marriage. I'm tired of trying to please everyone but myself." But I heard God say, "No, don't give up, I'll help you. Every time you have a negative thought, change it into a positive thought." So I started turning things from negative to positive. I started being grateful for the things I had. I started being grateful for life, health, my home, my business, my family, and my grandchildren. I still struggle to speak up, offer my opinions, or say what I'm thinking. I still fight the fear of failure, the fear of being laughed at, and the fear of not being able to talk intelligently. But God is working in me and through me. He helps me every step of the way.

Then It began to sink in: I am Loved, I am Beloved, and I have purpose. I am a daughter of the King, and people do want to hear what I have to say. I have a voice, and God has a plan for me. God revealed to me how to renew my mind and change my thinking. I realized just by changing my thinking, I could be happy in my circumstances. I have been happy since. Life around you, the people in your life, start changing a little at a time when you change your thinking. When you know your worth, who you are, and what you stand for, when you find your truth and start using your voice. And if I can only help one person who doesn't have a voice? That's what I want to do. If I can help you, if I can help you find your voice and start speaking up for yourself and find out who you are, what you think, and what your opinion is, I will. If you have lost yourself, discover your value, your worth, your contribution, your voice, your uniqueness, I will help you find this freedom. I would love to encourage and empower you to listen to yourself, to listen to who you are and what God has to say about you. Send me an e-mail, message me, or find me on Facebook. I can't wait to talk to you. I can't wait to hear your story. The story that God has changed your life, that you're finding yourself, you're finding your voice, and it's changing your life.

I finally heard the lesson! There were concrete actions I could take to find and use my voice to create the life I had dreamt about. Let me share those with you:

Focus, Transfer, Love.

Focus: What does God say about you? Describe it more.

> Ephesians 2:10 says I am God's masterpiece, I am New in Christ so that I can do the good things He planned for me long ago.

1. Ask yourself. Who am I? What is my purpose? Who does God say I am? What are my talents and gifts?
2. Write this information out and read it every day. Write affirmations to speak out loud every day.
3. Put them all over so you can read them anytime, day or night.

Transfer: Transfer a negative thought into a good and productive thought. (Transfer the "I can't, I don't, I won't" TO "I can, I will, and I do."

> When the negative would flood my mind, I would speak what I know is true.
>
> I am the daughter of the King.
>
> God's word says of me You will go out in Joy. You'll be led into a whole and complete life. Isaiah 55:12,
>
> God's plan for me is to prosper and have hope and a future. Jeremiah 29:11 I am made for a purpose.
>
> Romans 4:17 "Call those things which are not as though they are.

Love as Jesus loves.

> His love is unconditional.
>
> It is by His grace that we are saved; we do not earn it.
>
> Let us honor Him by loving others as He loves us.
>
> Change that judgment into understanding.
>
> Remember whose you are.
>
> Transfer those negative thoughts to true thoughts that God has spoken over you.

#FocusTransferLove

And most of all SPEAK LIFE

I feel safe
Content
Yet I feel unforgiveable
I cannot seem
To take the right step
Make the right choice
TV, Food, Laziness
Consume me
I hear You calling
I feel You drawing
Yet I am stuck
I long for Your Spirit to free me
Deliver me
Set me on fire
'See, I told you
No one cares
You are mine
I have got you stuck.'
But my God cares
I know it is true
Unstick me God
It is You I need
You are my Hope
What I want to do
And what I do
Are totally opposite
I cry out

I cry out
When will my help come?
I am paralyzed
God you are my Hope
Where my help comes from
Holy Spirit come
Fill me
Deliver me
Overcome me
I Know you love me
I know you care
I have felt Your Presence
And been Blessed
By Your Unchanging Love

Made in the USA
Middletown, DE
11 June 2023

32389607R00093